Revise BTEC National

Applied Psychology

Revision Guide

Series Consultant: Harry Smith

Authors: Nicole Driver and Susan Harty

A note from the publisher

While the publishers have made every attempt to ensure that advice on the qualification and its assessment is accurate, the official specification and associated assessment guidance materials are the only authoritative source of information and should always be referred to for definitive guidance.

This qualification is reviewed on a regular basis and may be updated in the future. Any such updates that affect the content of this Revision Guide will be outlined at **www.pearsonfe.co.uk/BTECchanges**. The eBook version of this Revision Guide will also be updated to reflect the latest guidance as soon as possible.

> **For the full range of Pearson revision titles across KS2, KS3, 11+, GCSE, Functional Skills, AS/A Level and BTEC visit:**
> www.pearsonschools.co.uk/revise

Published by Pearson Education Limited, 80 Strand, London, WC2R 0RL.

www.pearsonschoolsandfecolleges.co.uk

Copies of official specifications for all Pearson qualifications may be found on the website: qualifications.pearson.com

Text and illustrations © Pearson Education Ltd 2019
Typeset and illustrated by QBS Learning
Produced by QBS Learning
Cover illustration by Clementine Hope

The rights of Nicole Driver and Susan Harty to be identified as authors of this work have been asserted by them in accordance with the Copyright, Designs and Patents Act 1988.

First published 2019

24
10 9 8 7 6 5 4 3 2

British Library Cataloguing in Publication Data
A catalogue record for this book is available from the British Library

ISBN 978 1 292 27271 9

Printed and bound by CPI Group (UK) Ltd, Croydon, CR0 4YY

Acknowledgements

Photographs

(Key: t–top; b–bottom; c–centre; l–left; r–right)

123RF: PaylessImages 14, Dolgachov 97; **Alamy Stock Photo:** Steve Skjold 4, ART Collection 24r, The History Collection 24l, Roger Utting 31, True Images 78; **Shutterstock:** Sylvie Bouchard 5, Margouillat photo 7, Val Lawless 25, Shutterstock 26, 27, Dmitry Lobanov 32, Startraks 34, Pikselstock 57, Kseniia Vorobeva 69, Michaeljung 77, Pathdoc 80, Bruce Ellis 81, Wavebreakmedia 82, Mick Atkins 90, Stephen Coburn 92, Jim Barber 102.

Notes from the publisher
1. While the publishers have made every attempt to ensure that advice on the qualification and its assessment is accurate, the official specification and associated assessment guidance materials are the only authoritative source of information and should always be referred to for definitive guidance.

Pearson examiners have not contributed to any sections in this resource relevant to examination papers for which they have responsibility.

2. Pearson has robust editorial processes, including answer and fact checks, to ensure the accuracy of the content in this publication, and every effort is made to ensure this publication is free of errors. We are, however, only human, and occasionally errors do occur. Pearson is not liable for any misunderstandings that arise as a result of errors in this publication, but it is our priority to ensure that the content is accurate. If you spot an error, please do contact us at resourcescorrections@pearson.com so we can make sure it is corrected.

Websites
Pearson Education Limited is not responsible for the content of any external internet sites. It is essential for tutors to preview each website before using it in class so as to ensure that the URL is still accurate, relevant and appropriate. We suggest that tutors bookmark useful websites and consider enabling students to access them through the school/college intranet.

Introduction

Which units should you revise?

This Revision Guide has been designed to support you in preparing for the externally assessed units of your course. Remember that you won't necessarily be studying all the units included here – it will depend on the qualification you are taking.

BTEC National Qualification	Externally assessed units
Certificate	1 Psychological approaches and applications
Extended Certificate	1 Psychological approaches and applications
	3 Health psychology

Your Revision Guide

Each unit in this Revision Guide contains two types of pages, shown below.

Content pages help you revise the essential content you need to know for each unit.

Skills pages help you prepare for your exam or assessed task. Skills pages have a coloured edge and are shaded in the table of contents.

Use the **Now try this** activities on every page to help you test your knowledge and practise the relevant skills.

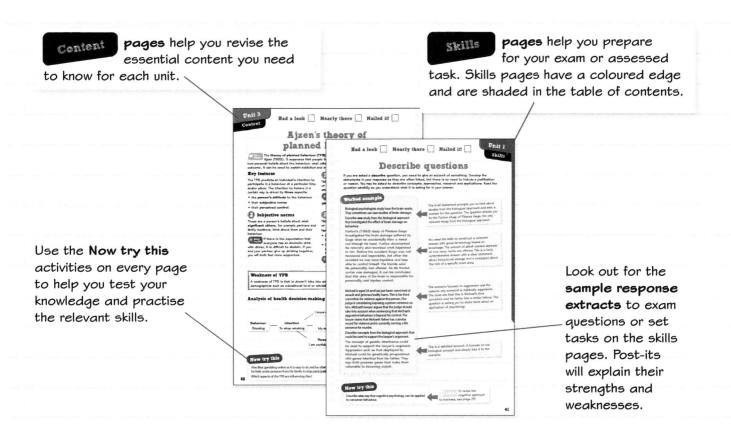

Look out for the **sample response extracts** to exam questions or set tasks on the skills pages. Post-its will explain their strengths and weaknesses.

Revising and applying key studies

When revising key studies:

- Consider each key study **in context** – for example, how it relates to the linked approach, concept, theory or area of psychology in the unit so you can select and evaluate studies to illustrate strengths and limitations or support your views.

- Consider how each key study can be **applied** to explain behaviour – for example, to different real-life situations and the relevant areas of focus in the unit. The **real world** feature gives some examples that you can use as prompts to think of different ways to apply studies and theories to the different areas of focus.

Contents

. . . .

A small bit of small print

Pearson publishes Sample Assessment Material and the Specification on its website. This is the official content and this book should be used in conjunction with it. The questions in Now try this have been written to help you test your knowledge and skills. Remember: the real assessment may not look like this.

Cognitive and social approaches

Psychological approaches include cognitive, social, learning (including behaviourism) and biological approaches. The key assumptions about **behaviour** for the **cognitive** and **social** approaches are revised here.

Cognitive approach

The cognitive approach in psychology explains behaviour as a product of the way the **mind processes** information about the world. The interaction between cognitive processes creates our experience of the world.

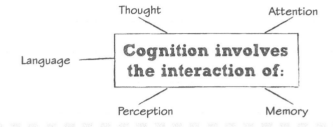

Language — **Cognition involves the interaction of:**
Thought   Attention   Perception   Memory

Cognitive approach assumptions

Here are **two** key assumptions of the cognitive approach.

1 Behaviour and information processing
Behaviour is a product of information processing. How individuals **think** affects how they **feel** and **react**. Belief systems impact on:

- the attention people pay to information
- how they store that information
- future interactions with the environment.

Real world If you **think** you cannot pass a test, you will **feel** powerless, and **react** so that you don't even try to succeed.

2 Input, processing and output
Information processing in the human mind works like a **computer** with **input, processing, storage** and **output** functions.

- Input is from our senses.
- Processing takes the form of thinking.
- Storage is memory.
- Output is behaviour.

Real world If you smell fresh bread baking (**input**), **processing** this information tells you it is tasty and to buy food (**output**).

Social approach

The social approach explains behaviour as a product of the social context in which it occurs. Humans are social animals, living in groups. We understand much behaviour in the context of our **socialisation**.

Social approach assumptions

Here are **two** key assumptions of the social approach.

1 Behaviour in a social context
Behaviour occurs in a social context. This means that individuals:

- are influenced by other people
- change their behaviour in accordance with the thoughts, opinions and actions of other people.

Real world You might sing with a group of friends on the way to a football match, but you would not do so alone.

2 Influence of culture and society
People's behaviour is influenced by other people, culture and society. Humans live in groups, so form societies with rules that influence behaviour that:

- include behavioural norms for groups
- are taught from birth so people are socialised to conform to the cultural norms
- greatly influence how people behave.

Real world Cultures have developed their own social norms for greetings, such as bowing or shaking hands.

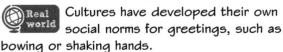

Now try this

Describe the social approach as it applies to psychology.

This is a straightforward question but requires more than a very brief outline – so include the two assumptions.

Learning and biological approaches

Psychological approaches include cognitive, social, learning (including behaviourism) and biological approaches. Here are the key assumptions about **behaviour** for the **learning** and **biological** approaches.

Learning approach

The learning approach suggests that who you are is a **product of learning** (nurture) and focuses on understanding the role of external environmental factors in the development of behaviour.

Learning approach assumptions

Here are **two** key assumptions of the learning approach.

1 **Behaviour is learned from the environment**

Behaviour is learned from experience of environmental stimuli. Conditioning happens when people associate events in the environment with outcomes and learn by the consequences of their actions.

Real world If you are sick after eating an egg sandwich, in future the smell of egg sandwiches might make you feel sick.

2 **Behaviour is learned from observation and imitation**

Behaviour is learned indirectly by people who:
- observe others interact with the environment
- imitate what other people do.

Real world If you watch a person eat an egg and have a negative reaction, you would be unlikely to want to eat an egg yourself.

Biological approach

The biological approach focuses on innate factors that influence behaviour (**nature**), rather than on what is learned from the environment (**nurture**).

Biological approach assumptions

Here are **two** key assumptions of the biological approach.

1 **Biological influences on behaviour**

Humans are biological beings.
- The organ of behaviour is the brain which, with the spinal cord, makes up the **central nervous system (CNS)**.
- **Genes** influence the structure of the brain.
- **Neurochemistry** regulates brain function.

Real world A person can inherit genes that predispose them to schizophrenia. Genes affect the brain's structure and its biochemistry, making some people susceptible to developing the symptoms of schizophrenia.

2 **Behaviour as a product of evolution**

Evolutionary pressures caused development of the human **genome**.
- Behaviour that was an adaptive advantage for human ancestors became part of the genetic code.
- The genetic code is passed on through the generations (survival of the fittest).

Real world Prehistoric humans were genetically programmed to respond to threats quickly.

'Nature versus nurture' is an important debate in psychology that concerns the relative contributions of inborn (biological) factors and environmental (learning) factors.

Now try this

Compare the views of a psychologist from the learning approach with those of one from the biological approach.

You need to consider what is different about the two approaches. The obvious difference is the view on nature verses nurture.

Reconstructive memory

🔑 **Key concept** Concepts from the **cognitive approach** include **reconstructive memory** and **schema**, and how these explain aspects of human behaviour. The concepts describe how humans organise, store and recall information.

Reconstructive memory

Bartlett (1932) proposed that memory is a dynamic process in which the memory of an event is reconstructed at the point of recall (see page 6). Our memories are unstable and adapt to new knowledge and experiences. This is influenced by schema development.

Role of schema

Schema are hypothetical mental frameworks of knowledge about specific concepts.

Schema develop throughout life as individuals gain experience of the world.

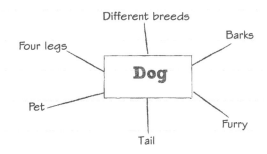

Here is a schema for our knowledge of dogs.

Schema development

The content of your schema affects what you pay attention to, and how you organise and store information. When you recall knowledge about something, the relevant schema is activated and its content affects how much and what you recall. This happens in **three** systematic ways.

1 Shortening

- People tend to remember the general idea of something rather than all the details.
- The key content is recalled, so when you recount your memory of an event, the recall is generally much shorter than the actual event.

2 Rationalisation

- Because your recall is based on what you already know, any new information is distorted to fit your picture of how the world works.
- You unconsciously change the new information in order to make sense of it.

3 Confabulation

- Because you don't recall every aspect of an event, you fill in the gaps using your existing schema.
- Sometimes you might recall things that did not actually happen. You merge your memory of the event with your existing schema in order to produce a more detailed version of what happened.

 Now try this

Milo is telling his friend Ben about a horror film he watched on TV. The film lasted two hours but Milo managed to convey the plot to Ben in only two minutes. He left out a lot of detail. Ben later tells another friend what the film is about, but includes a nasty ghost that did not actually appear in the film.

Explain Milo's loss of detail about the film, and why Ben remembered something that was not part of what Milo told him. Use your knowledge of schema to answer this question.

 Select the most appropriate schema development concepts to explain aspects of the scenario. Loss of detail links to **shortening**, and recall of events that did not happen links to **confabulation**.

Priming and cognitive scripts

 Concepts from the **cognitive approach** include **priming**. There are different types of priming, including repetitive, semantic and associative. Cognitive scripts are schema that are triggered (or primed for) in some situations and which also affect aspects of behaviour.

Role of cognitive scripts

Scripts are **schema** for actions that can be used to explain routine behaviour.

- They are triggered when individuals are in situations that require action.
- They develop with time and experience.

 When you enter a restaurant, you have a script of what to do and when to do it. You know the order in which behaviour is supposed to happen (by yourself and by others) and you respond accordingly.

Role of priming

Priming activates a relevant schema which affects your reaction to events in the environment. Priming can be:

- positive when a response is quick
- negative if it causes a slower response.

 When positively primed by a good smell in a restaurant, you quickly recognise food you like on the menu. When negatively primed by an unappetising picture on the menu, it takes longer to select food.

Repetitive priming

This is when you regularly experience something and it sets you up to respond to it more quickly in future. The more often you experience the prime followed by the situation, the faster the prime activates the relevant schema in future.

 In advertising, the product name and the product become linked by repetition. The name is enough to trigger recall of the product, and vice versa.

Here your cognitive script would prompt you to go to the counter to order, not sit at the table waiting to be served.

Semantic priming

Semantic priming is when:

- the prime and the target come from similar categories and share features
- thinking of a specific item within the category primes you to quickly process information about other members of the same category.

 Consumers could be primed to buy tulips by pictures of daffodils at the entrance to the shop.

Associative priming

Associative priming is when:

- the prime and the target are regularly experienced together
- the prime and the target are **not** from the same conceptual category.

 Some colours have specific associations, such as the colour green and environmental responsibility. Advertisers use green packaging to prime the idea that a product is environmentally friendly.

Now try this

Kath sells produce from her garden for donations. She often finds that there is less money in the box than expected. Her friend Ash suggests that she puts a notice on the box with a picture of eyes, because he says people are more law-abiding when they think they are being watched.

Explain why Ash's suggestion might be successful, using concepts from the cognitive approach.

 This question requires you to **explain**. You should read the information you are given carefully and give a reason why Ash's idea would work. The question specifies the **cognitive** approach, so you must select appropriately from those key concepts, such as priming.

Cognitive bias

🔑 **Key concept** Concepts from the **cognitive approach** include **cognitive bias**, which concerns the ways in which humans process information. A bias is faulty thinking that includes fundamental attribution error, confirmation bias and hostile attribution bias. Understanding bias allows us to explain how behaviour can be affected by faulty thinking.

Cognitive bias

Human minds develop short cuts for processing information about the world, especially social information. These short cuts:

- speed up our understanding, as they enable us to spot patterns
- help us act quickly
- often lead to errors or **cognitive biases**.

Psychologists have studied errors in thinking, or biases, in order to explain how they affect aspects of our behaviour.

Role of fundamental attribution error

The fundamental attribution error is a common error in thinking. People tend to:

- locate the cause of events in deliberate acts by others – blame the person not the situation when someone else is the actor
- underemphasise the role of deliberation in our own behaviour – blame the situation not ourselves when we are the actor.

🌐 **Real world** If we arrive late, we are likely to say we were busy, but if someone else is late we might think they are rude.

Role of confirmation bias

Confirmation bias is a frequent error in thinking. People tend to:

- pay attention to, and therefore recall, information that supports what they already know or think they know
- ignore disconfirming information that doesn't support what they know
- persist in holding mistaken beliefs, despite evidence that they are wrong.

🌐 **Real world** If you believe someone is not punctual, you will recall times when they were late but not when they were early.

Role of hostile attribution bias

Hostile attribution bias (HAB) is a personality characteristic that is stronger in some people than others. People with HAB:

- have a biased perception about the intentions of other people
- interpret signals from others as intentionally hostile
- often react to others with aggression.

For someone with HAB, even a neutral expression like this can be interpreted as being intentionally hostile, leading to an aggressive interaction.

Now try this

Pete is charged with grievous bodily harm. He attacked a man, causing him serious injury. He said the other man was 'disrespecting him and looking at him funny'. Witnesses said the victim was simply minding his own business and didn't interact with Pete.

Explain why Pete may have reacted in this way. Use your knowledge of cognitive bias to answer.

In this question the command word is **explain**, so you must give a reason for what you say.

Select the most appropriate cognitive bias to answer this question. Use direct quotes from the scenario to illustrate your answer.

The Bartlett study (1932)

 Key study 'War of the Ghosts' is a **cognitive approach** study in which Bartlett demonstrated the features of reconstructive memory in storytelling: shortening, rationalisation and confabulation.

Key principles

This is an early investigation into memory. It can be regarded more as a demonstration than a scientific study, unlike more recent research into memory. Bartlett's **aim** was to show how recall of a story became distorted with retelling, both immediately and after some time.

Procedure

1. British participants were told the 'War of the Ghosts', a native American folktale.

2. Some were immediately asked to tell the story to another person, who told it to someone else (to demonstrate serial reproduction).

3. Bartlett recorded each retelling.

4. Bartlett asked some participants to recall the story at various time intervals up to two years after they first heard it.

5. Again, he recorded the retelling.

Findings

1. **Shortening** was evident as each retelling got shorter than the last, both over time and in the serial reproduction.

2. **Rationalisation** happened as the story lost its original supernatural element and become an account of a fishing accident.

3. **Confabulation** occurred as elements of the story changed. For example, seal hunting (something for which British people are unlikely to have a schema) became fishing.

4. **Reconstruction of memory** was shown. Rather than just passively replaying the story, the participants actively reconstructed it from multiple sources.

Conclusions

Memory is fluid. Memory for a story changes over time, and at each recall it is affected by other information that is known (schema).

 Real world **Explaining behaviour**

The study has important application to the real world, such as in eyewitness testimony in police investigations, as it shows how recall from memory changes over time. Memory is not always reliable. For example, culturally specific schema can cause confabulation (see page 3).

Evaluating strengths and limitations of the study

Strengths	Limitations
👍 The findings of the study are consistent with other similar research, showing that the results are quite reliable and are a valid test of reconstructive memory.	👎 There was a lack of standardisation in the procedure, reducing reliability. For example, the intervals between recall events were not consistent, and the length of time the participants were exposed to the original story varied.
👍 The method has ecological validity as it tests recall for stories in a real-world way, rather than using the simplistic word lists that feature in most memory research.	👎 The study may lack population validity as it was tested only on British participants. Those from other cultures may have performed differently.

Now try this

State the findings of Bartlett's 'War of the Ghosts' study. The command in this question is **state**, so not much detail is required.

The Harris et al. study (2009)

Key study 'Priming effects of television food advertising on eating behavior' is a **cognitive approach** study by Harris, Bargh and Brownell. The researchers found a change in children's eating behaviour when TV adverts for junk food triggered eating schema.

Key principles

This study investigated the possible influence of schema and priming on eating behaviour. The **aim** was to investigate the effect of TV adverts on the consumption of snack food. Two similar experiments were conducted, one on children and another on young adults. The one using children most clearly demonstrates the effect of priming.

Procedure

1 Children were randomly allocated to a group that saw junk-food adverts or to a group that watched adverts for non-food products.

2 All children watched the same cartoon alone and were provided with the same snacks.

In the **findings**, researchers found that the children in the junk-food TV adverts group ate more snack food than those who did not see the adverts.

3 Researchers measured the amount of snack food consumed during the study by each child.

Conclusions

Junk-food adverts triggered schema for automatic eating habits, influencing food consumption.

Real world **Explaining behaviour**

The study has useful application as it shows how food advertising can affect consumption. This is important as there is a growing concern in society about childhood obesity. The study suggests that banning such adverts during programmes watched by children might be a useful intervention.

Evaluating strengths and limitations of the study

Strengths	Limitations
👍 The study used good controls, increasing validity. All children had an identical viewing experience except for the adverts they saw, so this is the only thing that could have caused the observed difference in food consumption.	👎 A criticism of the study might be that it lacks ecological validity because the setting was artificial – the children watched TV alone and unsupervised. It is possible that the adverts might have a different effect in a more social situation.
👍 Real-life adverts were used, increasing ecological validity.	👎 The study failed to establish the exact cause of the increase in junk-food consumption, reducing validity. The later experiment on young adults tested the effect of advertising healthy food against junk food and found no difference, just that food adverts in general increased consumption.

Now try this

With reference to Harris, Bargh and Brownell's findings, suggest why some people think junk-food adverts should be banned from children's TV.

Refer to priming and schema in your answer.

The Loftus and Palmer study (1974)

 Key study 'Reconstruction of automobile destruction' is a **cognitive approach** study that looked at how information provided after an event triggered schema in participants and influenced their recall. This can explain aspects of human memory.

Key principles

Two **laboratory experiments** investigated the effect of schema on memory. Their **aim** was to test the effect of leading (critical) questions on participants' recall of car crashes.

Procedure 1 and findings

1. Participants watched films of car crashes.

2. They completed questionnaires to test recall.

3. The leading question about speed at impact used one descriptor from: **contacted, bumped, hit, collided, smashed.**

4. In the **findings**, the participants' estimates of speed were affected by the descriptor. On average, those in the 'smashed' group recalled the speed as fastest. Those in the 'contacted' group recalled the speed as lowest.

Procedure 2 and findings

1. Participants watched films of car crashes.

2. They were asked how fast the cars were travelling as they **smashed** or **hit** each other.

3. One week later they were asked whether broken glass was seen at the site.

4. In the **findings**, the participants who were asked the 'smashed' question were more likely to recall seeing broken glass, even though none was shown (confabulation).

Conclusion

The word used to describe the impact between the cars affected recall of their speed. The descriptor activated schema – speed is relevant to the schema for 'smashed', causing the participant to recall that the car was travelling fast, or to add false details about broken glass.

🌐 Real world Explaining behaviour

The study has useful application in understanding human behaviour as it shows how the wording of a question can affect recall for an event. Police are careful not to use leading questions that may influence witnesses when gathering eyewitness statements of crimes.

Evaluating strengths and limitations of the study

Strengths	Limitations
👍 Both studies used controlled laboratory conditions. The only variation between the groups was the leading question's descriptor word. This is the only thing that could have caused the difference in participants' recall, so the experiments were valid and reliable.	👎 It could be argued that the studies lack ecological validity. There was no consequence for a wrong answer, so participants may have been more susceptible to leading questions. In a real situation, witness recall of a car crash might result in prosecution of the driver.
👍 The application of this research means that police use careful wording in questions so they do not influence eyewitness recall. This can help prevent false convictions based on inaccurate eyewitness testimony and false details from confabulation.	👎 Participants were students, possibly lacking driving experience, so generalisability was low. Lack of experience could make them more vulnerable to bias from the wording of the question compared to more experienced people.

Now try this

Loftus and Palmer found that recall of speed differed depending on the word used to describe the crash.

Explain this difference in the recall of speed using your knowledge of schema.

 This is asking you to explain the results. You should focus on schema.

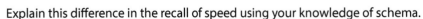

Social conformity

 Key concept Concepts from the **social approach** include **conformity**. Normative and informational social influence make us more or less likely to conform to group behaviour and attitudes, explaining aspects of our behaviour.

Conformity

Conformity happens when people change their attitudes, beliefs or behaviour to that of the group. Conformity operates at **three** different levels and is caused by different influences.

1 Compliance

This is the shallowest level of conformity. The person simply goes along with the group without any real conversion to their ideas. This is a temporary public change but not a genuine private change.

 Some people might avoid using plastic bottles when with their friends but use them when their friends are not present.

2 Identification

This level of conformity is linked to group values. To be part of the group, people adopt group values. Change is longer lasting, public and private, but may fade when group membership is no longer important.

 If a person becomes friends with environmentalists, they might change their attitude about plastic bottles while they are with the group. If they leave, this attitude could fade.

3 Internalisation

This is the deepest level of conformity and it involves a public and private change that is likely to be permanent. The change persists outside the context of group membership.

 If someone truly believes that plastic bottles are environmentally unfriendly, their attitude change will be permanent and independent of who they are with.

Role of normative social influence

Normative social influence involves:

- changing behaviour to the group norms to fit in with them and be accepted by the group
- change that is likely to be shallow and short term.

 In this case, an individual might reject the use of plastic bottles when in the company of one group of environmentally conscious friends, but use them when with friends who think differently.

Role of informational social influence

Informational social influence involves:

- changing to the group norm when the group has knowledge that the person doesn't
- changing to behave, think or feel like the group members
- change that is deep and long-lasting.

 If an individual learns about how plastics damage the environment, they might change their behaviour to try to stop using plastic completely.

Now try this

Amita gets a new job. On her first day, she wears casual clothes but the other staff members wear suits. She buys a suit and wears it the next day, even though it feels uncomfortable.

1 Identify the type of social influence that Amita is experiencing.
2 Justify your answer.

This is a two-part question.
- The first part is to identify the type of social influence affecting Amita. This requires you to name the right one.
- The second part requires you to explain why you chose that type. To do this you will need to use information from the scenario.

Social categorisation

 Key concept Concepts from the **social approach** include **social categorisation** and how this explains aspects of human behaviour. The formation and effects of social categories, or stereotypes, merge social psychology with cognition because stereotypes involve schema.

Social categorisation

Humans organise information into categories.

- People classify each other based on certain characteristics.
- How individuals classify others influences what they think they know about them and how they act towards them.

 Real world Someone on your course scores highly on tests, doesn't use social media and rarely joins in banter. You categorise them as a 'nerd' and don't interact. You don't find out about their cool hobby.

Types of categorisation

There are many types of social categories. How we apply these varies from person to person, but there are some basic categories that most people seem to use:

- **age** – for example, baby, child, young, middle-aged, old, retired
- **gender** – such as male, female, transsexual, non-binary
- **occupation** – for example, psychologist, teacher, delivery driver, shop worker, volunteer.

Formation of stereotypes

A stereotype is a social schema that contains information about a specific category.

People form stereotypes when:

- they categorise others
- the category becomes associated with certain general characteristics.

 Real world The stereotypical student would be young, have limited money and not like getting up in the mornings.

Effect of stereotypes

Stereotypes affect how people think about and behave towards others.

- Individuals make **assumptions** about people based on the categories they put them in.
- These assumptions may be totally wrong but affect how people interact.

 Real world Before meeting a student you might assume they are young, at college and aiming for a career, whereas they could be older, and at home doing a distance-learning course for personal interest.

Problems of stereotyping

Although stereotypes usually have some truth in them, they:

- make generalisations and are inaccurate
- cause individuals to generate **biased** pictures of others.

 Real world A stereotype for a nurse might include characteristics of being caring and helpful, and it could be surprising to meet a grumpy one who doesn't fit the stereotype.

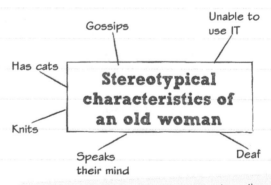

Do these characteristics actually describe the older women that you know?

Now try this

Liam is meeting his girlfriend's father, Jim, a builder, for the first time. Liam brings a gift of some beer. However, Jim does not drink alcohol.

Explain why Liam chose beer as a gift, using the concepts of social categorisation and stereotyping.

 This question asks for an explanation of Liam's choice using **both** social categorisation and stereotyping. Make sure that both are included in the answer.

The Asch study (1951)

> 🔍 **Key study** 'Effects of group pressure upon the modification and distortion of judgments' is a **social approach** study by Asch. It is an experimental investigation into social conformity to the majority view.

Key principles

Asch looked at conformity to a group. He used a controlled environment to test the extent to which individuals conform to an obviously wrong answer given by the rest of the group.

Procedure

1 A sample of American male undergraduates was recruited, they thought for a vision test.

2 Each one was put into a small group of people and tested 18 times. All other group members were Asch's **confederates** (actors) with instructions on how to behave.

3 The participants had to say which of the lines – A, B or C – matched the standard line X. The real participant was always last or second to last in the group.

4 In 12 out of 18 trials (the **critical trials**), the confederates all gave the same wrong answer.

5 The researcher measured the number of times the real participant conformed to the group.

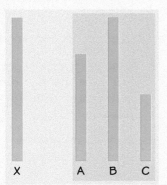

In the experiment, the participants had to say which of the lines A, B or C matched the standard line X.

Findings

1 Three-quarters of participants conformed at least some of the time to the obviously incorrect view expressed by the actors.

2 Around one-third of the critical trials showed conformity.

3 Very few of the participants never conformed.

Conclusions

Some participants who conformed:

- described **normative social influence** – feeling uncomfortable in going against the group. Asch called not wanting to stand out from the group a **distortion of behaviour**

- showed a **distortion of perception**, saying they believed others were seeing something they didn't and so conformed due to **informational social influence**.

> 🌐 **Real world** ## Explaining behaviour

In 1950s America, conforming to the majority view was a very strong social norm. This may explain why Asch found high levels of conformity to a wrong answer in a social setting.

Evaluating strengths and limitations of the study

Strengths	Limitations
👍 The standardised and controlled procedure meant few extraneous variables affected the results, improving reliability and internal validity.	👎 **Ecological validity** was poor. Giving a wrong answer had no consequences, maybe leading to more conformity than in the real world.
👍 Measurement of conformity was objective, meaning that there was no chance of researcher bias, and improving reliability of the data.	👎 Participants were unrepresentative as all were young males from a specific time period. Other groups in different times and places in society may act differently.

 Now try this

Describe the procedure used by Asch in his study of conformity.

 Notice the focus here is only on the procedure.

11

The Chatard et al. study (2007)

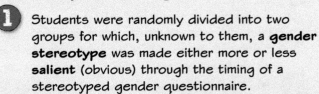 **Key study** The **social approach study, 'How good are you in math? The effect of gender stereotypes on students' recollection of their school marks'** by Chatard, Guimond and Selimbegovic involved two experiments into the impact of stereotypes on students' perception of their own academic abilities.

Key principles

Gender stereotyping is deep-rooted – it affects not only how people view others, but also how they see themselves. The **aim** of the study was to investigate the effect of common stereotypes on the perceived academic ability of males and females.

Preliminary study and findings

1 French high school students indicated their agreement or otherwise with four statements about gender and academic ability.

2 Students recalled their previous scores in important standardised maths and arts tests.

3 In the **findings**, students who held stereotypes about male and female academic ability tended to recall their own academic abilities as being similar to the stereotypes.

Conclusions

Gender stereotypes affected students' perception of their abilities, leading to bias in the reporting of their own test marks.

This causes potential problems for society as people are restricted by gender stereotypes.

Main study and findings

1 Students were randomly divided into two groups for which, unknown to them, a **gender stereotype** was made either more or less **salient** (obvious) through the timing of a stereotyped gender questionnaire.

Low salience	High salience
1 Rate own ability	**1** Gender questionnaire
2 Gender questionnaire	**2** Rate own ability
3 Recall own test score	**3** Recall own test score

2 The data consisted of the difference between the participants' recall of maths and arts test scores with their actual scores.

3 In the high salience **findings**, there was underestimation by girls of their maths ability and underreporting of arts scores by boys compared to low salience conditions.

Real world Explaining behaviour

The study has useful application as it highlights the negative effect of stereotypes. It suggests that stereotypes can result in 'self-fulfilling prophecies' so females choose not to study maths and science because they believe they are unable to do well.

Evaluating strengths and limitations of the study

Strengths	Limitations
👍 The study was well controlled. The data were based on objectively measured scores of ability (the standardised tests).	👎 The student sample may not be representative. Older people may be less affected by stereotypes.
👍 There was a reasonably sized sample from which to generalise, increasing population validity.	👎 Students knew about the study and may have guessed its aims. **Demand characteristics** could affect data if scores were recalled to support the hypothesis, reducing validity.

Now try this

Explain how people's life chances can be affected by gender stereotypes. Refer to this study in your answer.

 This question is about how stereotypes influence people's beliefs about achievement.

The Haney et al. study (1973)

🔍 Key study 'A **study of prisoners and guards in a simulated prison**' by Haney, Banks and Zimbardo is one of the most famous **social approach** studies in psychology, and has even been the subject of feature films. Professor Zimbardo led this Stanford prison study, which looks at the effect of social roles on behaviour.

Key principles

Although often referred to as an experiment, this study was a **controlled observation**. It gathered qualitative (descriptive) data about behavioural change in a social situation. The **aim** was to investigate how being given a specific social role of prisoner or guard affects behaviour.

Procedure

1 Participants answered an advert for a study on prison life. They were screened for potential mental health and other issues.

2 A mock-up of a prison was constructed.

3 Participants were randomly allocated to the role of prisoner or guard.

4 The 'guards' were given training and a uniform. The 'prisoners' were 'arrested', and given prison clothes and numbers.

5 Zimbardo and his colleagues acted as superintendent and prison officers. They recorded the behaviour as it happened.

Findings

1 The guards became abusive, as they enforced rules and humiliated the prisoners.

2 The prisoners became passive and some experienced mental distress.

Ethics

The study was stopped after six days due to the deteriorating condition of the prisoners. A code of ethical guidelines was developed in response to this and other social studies, so that research plans now have to be approved by an ethics committee.

Conclusions

Participants conformed to the norms of their social roles. They identified with their group and their behaviour changed, showing how behaviour is changed by social norms based on social expectations.

🌐 Real world Explaining behaviour

The study has useful application as it shows how social situation affects behaviour. It helps to explain how abuse can happen in prison situations. Zimbardo was an expert witness in defence of American soldier guards who were accused of abusing prisoners in Abu Ghraib in Iraq.

Evaluating strengths and limitations of the study

Strengths	Limitations
👍 Evidence suggests the scenario was very realistic (prisoners referred to themselves by number, even when not being observed), indicating high experimental validity.	👎 There were ethical issues – the participants were not protected from psychological harm. Some prisoners suffered extreme stress and some guards were upset that they could have behaved so badly.
👍 We can be reasonably sure it was the social roles that caused the differences in behaviour. The participants were screened for psychological abnormalities before the study and were randomly allocated roles.	👎 Zimbardo was criticised for lacking objectivity as he became immersed in the role of superintendent and lost sight of the effects on participants. He became a **biased observer** so data may have been affected.

Now try this

Assess the Haney, Banks and Zimbardo prison study, in terms of **one** strength **and one** weakness.

 This question is asking you to evaluate the study. You could use 'however' between the strength and weakness to link your points.

Classical conditioning

 Key concept Concepts from the **learning approach** include **classical conditioning** and how this explains aspects of human behaviour. Classical conditioning involves direct learning through association of events within the environment.

Learning by association

Classical conditioning proposes that people learn to associate a **stimulus in the environment** with an automatic **reflex response** to create new behaviour patterns. **Five** points explain how.

1 Neutral stimulus (NS)

There are things in the environment for which humans have no natural reflex response. These don't usually affect behaviour.

 Real world Normally, seeing a feather (NS) wouldn't change someone's behaviour.

2 Unconditioned stimulus (UCS)

An unconditioned stimulus is an environmental stimulus that naturally causes a reflex response in humans.

 Real world People show fear when startled by an unexpected loud noise (UCS).

3 Unconditioned response (UCR)

An unconditioned response is an automatic and unlearned reflex response to an unconditioned stimulus.

 Real world The startle reflex, a fearful response to a loud noise, is a UCR.

4 Conditioned stimulus (CS)

If a neutral stimulus is paired with an unconditioned stimulus often enough or with sufficient emotional impact, the two stimuli become associated until the neutral stimulus automatically causes the same response as the unconditioned stimulus. When it does, it becomes a conditioned stimulus.

 Real world If a person is repeatedly and consistently presented with a feather (NS) at the same time as a loud bang (UCS), eventually the feather alone (CS) causes a fear response, such as a flinch.

5 Conditioned response (CR)

When a person shows the same response to the neutral stimulus without the unconditioned stimulus being present, they have **learned** to respond. This is a conditioned response.

 Real world If, every time a person sees a feather (CS) they flinch with fear (CR), they have been conditioned.

Pteronophobia is the proper name for an extreme fear of feathers. This and other phobias are often learned responses.

Summary of stages of conditioning

The process of classical conditioning can be divided into three stages of learning that show the effect of associating the stimulus and response:

1	Pre-learning	UCS → UCR
2	Learning	NS + UCS → UCR
3	Learned	CS → CR

Now try this

As a child, Amina watched a clown entertainer. During the show, a balloon popped nearby, causing her distress. Now she feels very anxious when she sees a clown.

Explain why Amina has a fear of clowns. Use your knowledge of classical conditioning to answer this question.

 This question specifies that you use classical conditioning in your answer. You should make sure that you can use the correct terminology. You could use a table or diagram like the one on this page to help you get the process right.

Operant conditioning

🔑 **Key concept**   Concepts from the **learning approach** include **operant conditioning** – learning through consequences such as reinforcement and punishment.

Learning by consequences

Operant conditioning states that people learn to change their behaviour as a result of the consequences of their actions. This can happen in **three** ways:

1 repeating actions that are directly **rewarded** (positive reinforcement)

2 repeating behaviours that **avoid** punishment (negative reinforcement)

3 deliberately not repeating actions that are **punished** (punishment).

① Positive reinforcement

Some actions produce a **direct reward**. A reward is a positive reinforcement, so the action is likely to be repeated in the future.

🌐 **Real world**   In a token economy, for example in a prison, rewards are controlled. Prisoners are conditioned to behave well in order to get positive reinforcements.

> Star charts are used to shape children's behaviour. By reinforcing desired behaviour with a star, the likelihood of the child repeating the behaviour is increased.

Star Chart

Name: Anna

	Monday	Tuesday	Wednesday	Thursday	Friday	Saturday	Sunday
I will brush my teeth	★	★					
I will finish my homework	★	★					
I will be kind	★	★ ★					
I will eat some fruit and veg	★						

② Negative reinforcement

Some actions are rewarding because they **avoid** a punishment. The behaviour is negatively reinforced, so is repeated.

🌐 **Real world**   You probably hand in your homework on time to avoid being told off.

③ Punishment

Some actions lead to unpleasant consequences. People are less likely to repeat behaviours that lead to punishments.

🌐 **Real world**   If grounded for coming home very late, you may not do it again.

Operant conditioning in animals

This concept suggests that behaviour in animals, as well as in humans, can be shaped and maintained by controlling consequences.

🌐 **Real world**   Operant conditioning is used extensively in animal training programmes, such as for assistance dogs. Desired behaviour, such as finding specific objects, is shaped by positive reinforcement (such as food treats).

Skinner's work

Skinner (1932) gradually shaped the behaviour of rats and pigeons to perform new actions by reinforcing approximations of the desired actions (see page 19). Every time the animal performed an action similar to the desired one they were reinforced, either positively or negatively, until they voluntarily produced the behaviour.

Now try this

Viktor gambles on slot machines. He enjoys winning money and keeps repeating the same behaviour. A psychologist suggested he gambles due to operant conditioning.

Suggest how the psychologist would explain Viktor's gambling behaviour.

 Use the key concept of reinforcement to explain why Viktor gambles.

Social learning theory

🔑 **Key concept** Concepts from the **learning approach** include **social learning theory**, which states that we learn through observing (watching) what others do and from what happens to them as a result of their actions. This explains aspects of human behaviour.

Learning through observation

Humans are social animals who:

- thrive in groups
- are naturally inclined to watch what other people do
- tend to focus more on human action and interaction than on any other aspect of the environment.

Imitation

Once behaviour has been observed, it can be copied. If you find yourself in a social situation similar to one you have observed, and you are capable of doing so, you may imitate the participants' behaviours.

🌐 **Real world** If a child witnesses a parent swear when they trip up, the child may also swear when they experience a similar event.

Modelling

Modelling is:

- **imitative** – we base our behaviour on the actions of other people
- **selective** – because we identify strongly with some people and are more likely to copy them.

🌐 **Real world** If a child witnesses a parent who is the same sex as them swear, they are more likely to identify with them and copy their behaviour.

the **consequence** for the role model of their action

the observer's **similarity** to the role model

Modelling behaviour depends on:

whether the observer is **capable** of replicating the role model's behaviour

the **status** of the role model

Modelling and reinforcement

Operant conditioning plays a part in modelling, because learning is stronger when the imitated action is directly reinforced (rewarded).

🌐 **Real world** If a child imitates a parent by swearing, this may make the parent laugh. Since this is a positive outcome for the child, they are being positively reinforced for swearing and are more likely to swear again.

Vicarious reinforcement

When a model's behaviour has positive consequences for them, it is more likely to be imitated by an observer. So if a model is rewarded for their behaviour, the observer is more likely to copy it than if the model is punished or if it causes no reaction.

🌐 **Real world** If one child sees another child imitate a parent by swearing and the parent laughs, the observing child is likely to copy the swearing.

Now try this

Jess is the mother of Dan, aged seven, and three-year-old twins, Ben and Jade. Jess has noticed that if Dan is doing something, Ben is more likely to copy his behaviour than Jade is. Jess saw that when she praised Dan for being kind and playing with his little sister, Ben also started to play with Jade.

Explain why Ben changes his behaviour to be similar to Dan's behaviour. Use your knowledge of social learning to answer this question.

The question is asking for an explanation of the youngest male child's behaviour, which he is modelling on his big brother. It specifies social learning theory so you have to select the most appropriate concepts for the scenario.

The Bandura et al. study (1961)

Key study 'Transmission of aggression through imitation of aggressive models' is a **learning approach** study by Bandura et al. that illustrates some of the key concepts of social learning theory, including observation, modelling and imitation.

Key principles

This study uses an observational technique within the method of a laboratory experiment. It has a complex procedure which is simplified and summarised below. Bandura et al.'s **aim** was to test the principles of social learning by investigating whether young children are likely to copy a model who behaves aggressively towards toys.

Procedure

1 Bandura et al. recruited pre-school children.

2 They were separated into groups based on gender, balancing their personality types.

3 The children watched an adult (male or female) playing either aggressively or non-aggressively with toys.

4 Mild frustration was aroused in the children by preventing them playing with some toys.

5 They were then left alone in a room with more toys, and their behaviour was observed.

Findings

1 Children were more likely to show aggression when they saw an adult behave aggressively.

2 More than half of the recorded aggressive acts came from the children who saw an aggressive adult.

3 The children were more likely to imitate the behaviour of the same-sex model.

4 Overall, boys were more physically aggressive than girls in every condition.

Conclusions

This study supports the claims of social learning theory because the children modelled their behaviour on higher status adults with similar gender characteristics to their own. They learned to interact aggressively with the toys because they observed what the adults did.

 Real world **Explaining behaviour**

The findings have useful application to society. If children imitate even unfamiliar adults, they are also likely to imitate actors on TV. This means programmes that are likely to be watched by children should avoid anti-social behaviour.

Evaluating strengths and limitations of the study

Strengths	Limitations
👍 The study is reliable because of the controls used: groups were matched in terms of personalities and so the main reason for aggressive or non-aggressive play was exposure to the model.	👎 The conclusion that children's aggression resulted from social learning is challenged because boys showed more aggression, despite having the same learning situation as girls. This suggests biological predisposition may affect aggression.
👍 A standardised procedure was used, making the experiment easy to replicate to test reliability.	👎 Pre-schoolers may be especially vulnerable to social learning, so findings may not generalise to other population sections.

Now try this

Bandura et al.'s study concluded that children are likely to show the effects of social learning.

Justify this claim, using your knowledge of the results of this study.

 This question is asking you to do more than simply describe the study. You need to understand the results and the claims of social learning theory, and then match them together.

The Watson and Rayner study (1920)

Key study 'Conditioned emotional reactions' is a **learning approach** study that demonstrates the effects of classical conditioning in a small child called 'Little Albert'.

Key principles

This was a controlled laboratory investigation. It had a single participant and was conducted over several weeks. Watson and Rayner's **aim** was to demonstrate that it was possible to create a fear response in an infant using the principles of classical conditioning (page 14), and to generalise the response from one object to other similar objects.

Procedure

1. **Establishing the baseline** – at about 11 months old, Albert was shown a variety of objects, including a rat, and was also subjected to a loud noise. He was afraid of the noise.

2. **Conditioning phase** – on several occasions, Albert was shown the rat while being exposed to the loud noise. He showed fear.

3. **Results of conditioning** – the rat was presented but not the noise. Albert still showed fear. He was conditioned to fear rats.

4. Albert was shown a range of objects which share some characteristics with rats, from a rabbit to a fur coat. He showed fear.

Conclusion

Albert learned to fear the rat through the process of classical conditioning, as summarised in the table.

Findings

1. At the start of the experiment Albert wasn't afraid of the rat – it was a neutral stimulus (NS). He was afraid of the noise which caused an unconditioned fear response (UCR).

2. The rat became associated with something that did naturally cause fear – the noise was the unconditioned stimulus (UCS).

3. Eventually, the rat acquired the power to cause fear – the conditioned response (CR). The rat, initially a neutral stimulus, became a conditioned stimulus (CS).

4. Albert's response was generalised to objects with similarities to rats.

Stage 1		UCS = noise	UCR = fear
Stage 2	NS = rat	UCS = noise	UCR = fear
Stage 3		CS = rat	CR = fear

Summary of conditioning process

Real world   Explaining behaviour

This study showed that classical conditioning can be applied to humans, and explained the development of some phobias. The phobic object becomes associated with something that naturally causes fear. This knowledge has led to successful phobia treatment.

Evaluating strengths and limitations of the study

Strengths	Limitations
👍 Exposure to the rat was controlled and Albert's reactions were measured at each stage. The procedure was reliable and valid. We can assume the change in his response to the rat resulted from experimental manipulation, showing classical conditioning.	👎 There are ethical concerns by modern standards. It was morally wrong to put Albert into a situation where he was likely to be psychologically damaged. Indeed, he is said to have left the study with a rat phobia.
👍 This study led to a successful explanation for phobias and also to treatment based on deconditioning the person so that they no longer fear the object.	👎 The study lacks ecological validity because of the systematic way Albert was exposed to the stimuli. In the real world, we are not conditioned in such a controlled way.

Now try this

Describe how the Watson and Rayner study can be applied to explain classical conditioning.

 Relate the study's findings to the model of classical conditioning.

The Skinner study (1932)

 Key study 'On the rate of formation of a conditioned reflex' is a series of **learning approach** studies in which Skinner demonstrated operant conditioning in animals.

Key principles

Skinner used rats and pigeons in his research with apparatus called a Skinner box. Skinner's **aim** was to refine his theory of operant conditioning by establishing the principles of **positive** and **negative reinforcement** of behaviour. He showed that reinforced behaviour is repeated.

Procedure

1. A rat, in a Skinner box for the first time, showed natural exploratory behaviour.

2. Skinner put food into the dispenser when the rat was in the lever area of the box.

3. Subsequently, he only released food when the rat was close to the lever.

4. Eventually, the rat pressed the lever and food was released (positive reinforcement).

5. Additionally, Skinner was able to shock the animal by applying an electric current to the floor. The rat could turn off the current by pressing the lever (negative reinforcement).

Findings

1. Initially, rats took time to press the lever.

2. When they had been in the box for a long time, or on several different occasions, they located and pressed the lever much faster.

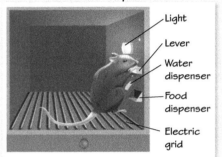

Light
Lever
Water dispenser
Food dispenser
Electric grid

A Skinner box is a controlled environment where behaviours can be selectively rewarded or punished.

Conclusions

Animals learn through the consequences of their actions.

- If rewarded for displaying a particular action, it is positively reinforced, so they repeat the behaviour.
- If avoiding an unpleasant situation, that action is negatively reinforced, so they repeat the behaviour.

 Real world **Explaining behaviour**

Skinner's research has useful application to human issues. For example, reinforcement of desired behaviour in prisons using tokens that can be exchanged for items of value reduces anti-social actions. Positive reinforcement is also used extensively in schools.

Evaluating strengths and limitations of the study

Strengths	Limitations
👍 The use of laboratory-raised animals means there was little chance that prior experience affected their behaviour, so changes in behaviour must be a product of learning through operant conditioning.	👎 The use of animals limits generalisation to humans. Rats have less developed cognitive functions and may be more affected by environmental pressures than humans, who can think about and change their behaviour.
👍 The scientific method used by Skinner was controlled and standardised, so reliability and validity were high.	👎 The research was unethical by modern standards. Skinner found underfed and hungry animals learned best.

Now try this

Jamal and Melissa have been asked to write a proposal to replicate Skinner's study.

Describe the aim and procedure of the study in sufficient detail to allow them to create a proposal.

This question is asking you to state facts about the study. Do this in a logical sequence that demonstrates the procedure.

19

Biology and behaviour

🔑 **Key concept** The **biological approach** is concerned with the influence of nature, in terms of inherited physiology, on human behaviour. Concepts from the biological approach, including **genetics** and **neurobiology**, explain behaviour as a function of biology.

Genetic terminology

Genes are units of inheritance that programme cell development in the body. **Genotype** is:

- all the genes that are present from conception and which drive development
- the genes inherited from both parents.

Phenotype is:

- the physical appearance of the organism
- the physiological result of our genes and their interaction with the environment.

 Real world Our genotype sets a possible height range (nature). How tall we grow in this range (our phenotype) depends on nutrition (nurture).

Genes and behaviour

Much of human behaviour is due to **genetic inheritance**.

- Males inherit a Y chromosome, which contains masculine genes, from their father.
- These genes initiate the development of masculine characteristics in the foetus, including male sex organs and genitalia.
- It also leads to the release of testosterone, a hormone which masculinises the developing foetal brain.

 Real world Prenatal exposure to testosterone is linked to aggression, showing how biology influences behaviour.

Neurochemistry

Brain chemistry is an important concept in psychology. Cells in the brain and body communicate via chemicals called neurotransmitters and hormones.

- **Neurotransmitters** are the chemical messengers of the CNS. Normal brain function requires a balance of these chemicals.

 Real world Depression has been linked to low levels of a neurotransmitter called serotonin, and schizophrenia to a possible excess of another called dopamine.

- **Hormones** are chemicals that are transported in the bloodstream. They are released by glands in the body and affect behaviour in many ways.

 Real world Sex hormones link to the reproductive organs. These affect mood and behaviour, as well as reproductive function.

Neuroanatomy and behaviour

The brain is the organ of behaviour. Its organisation affects how we behave.

- There are two hemispheres, each with four regions called lobes.
- Some cognitive functions are associated with specific locations. For example, decision-making is mainly located in the frontal lobes.
- Damage to some areas of the brain affects how we think, feel and behave.

MALE FEMALE

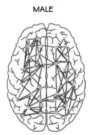 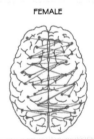

Male brains are organised for communication **within** each hemisphere, whereas female brains are organised for communication **between** the hemispheres.

Now try this

Compare the views of the biological approach (nature) to those of the learning approach (nurture) (see page 2). Focus on the way that each explains behaviour.

 You need to focus on an aspect of one approach and clearly explain the way in which that aspect is different in the other. Use an effective linking word to start the comparison such as 'whereas'.

Evolutionary psychology

🔑 **Key concept** The concept of evolutionary psychology, including ideas of adaptation, survival of the fittest, sexual selection and genome lag, underpins the whole of the **biological approach**. All behaviour with a genetic component has evolved.

Theory of evolution

Individual organisms compete for resources.

- If they are successful competitors they survive and reproduce, passing their genes to the next generation.
- Some genes make an organism a better fit for the environment, prolonging life and increasing reproductive opportunities (**survival of the fittest**).
- Genes that have no advantage or are a disadvantage are less likely to be inherited.

 Real world Giraffes have evolved long necks to eat leaves from tall trees.

Evolution of behaviour

Genes are the units of inheritance (see page 20). They affect behaviour through their influence on physiology and brain biology. Rarely, genes change through random genetic **mutation**.

- This gives offspring slightly different genes from parents.
- If a new pattern of genes helps the offspring survive, the genes are likely to be passed on to the next generation.
- If the new pattern of genes gives a behavioural change which is advantageous, the new behaviour will be inherited.

Environment of evolutionary adaptation

According to this theory, in order to survive, an organism has to fit the environment. A change in the environment could mean that different genes become more successful.

 Real world In human terms, the **environment of evolutionary adaptation** existed many thousands of years ago. Our fight-or-flight response evolved in the context of prehistoric dangers. Now we experience this response when we are stressed (see page 75).

If food becomes scarce, the giraffe with a genetic mutation for a slightly longer neck will be better suited to the environment.

Sexual selection

This process is driven by reproduction.

- Males and females are needed to produce offspring.
- Both sexes choose the best mate.
- Choosing the best mate increases the chance that the offspring will survive and pass on their genes.

🌐 **Real world** Female red deer select and mate with stags that demonstrate their superior strength in display fights called ruts.

Genome lag

Environments change faster than genes, especially since humans started to shape the world to their own needs. However, humans still have the same genes that developed in the environment of evolutionary adaptation, so our genes suit the past and not the present.

🌐 **Real world** Men prefer to partner with younger (and therefore more fertile) females, even though there is no longer evolutionary pressure to produce many offspring.

Now try this

'Fight-or-flight' is an innate response to threat. When threatened, the body and brain prepare to fight or run away. This was advantageous in prehistoric times when danger was physical, but is now problematic as many threats are psychological.

Explain why humans still have the fight-or-flight response.

This question is asking you to explain genome lag but in the context of a specific behaviour (fight-or-flight).

The Buss et al. study (1992)

🔍 **Key study** 'Sex differences in jealousy: evolution, physiology, and psychology' is a **biological approach** study that investigated differences in sexual jealousy between men and women and related findings to evolutionary theories about reproductive behaviour.

Key principles

This study used a theoretical dilemma to prompt participants to reflect on their reactions to an unfaithful partner. The **aim** was to explore differences in sexual jealousy between males and females, and to consider whether evolution could explain these.

- A similar **second experiment** measured physiological signs of distress.
- A related **third experiment** looked at the effect of previous relationships on jealousy.

Procedure

1. Students were asked to think of a real or imagined committed romantic relationship.

2. They had to say how they would react if their partner became involved, emotionally or sexually, with someone else.

3. Finally, there were questions about a partner trying new sexual positions or falling in love with another person. Data consisted of a measure of reported distress.

Findings and conclusions

1. **Men** reported and showed more distress at the thought of their partner being sexually unfaithful.

2. **Women** reported and showed more distress at the thought of their partner being emotionally unfaithful.

Buss et al. concluded that men and women have different reactions to infidelity due to the evolution of sexual behaviour.

🌐 Real world Explaining behaviour

Buss et al. claimed their results support evolutionary theory.

- **Males** were distressed by potentially losing the rights to their partner's fertility. In biological terms, the risk to the male of his partner's infidelity is another man making her pregnant, denying him the opportunity to pass on his genes.

- **Females** were concerned by emotional infidelity. To pass on her genes in the environment of evolutionary adaptation, the female needed resources from the male (food and protection), which were secured when the male formed a deep attachment to her.

Evaluating strengths and limitations of the study

Strengths	Limitations
👍 The method controlled for reliability by using a questionnaire. All participants got the same information. There was no bias in the way males and females were treated.	👎 Students may have strong social norms about relationships, causing validity issues. If participants express those rather than their own feelings, data will be inaccurate.
👍 The three experiments used different measurements but gave similar results, increasing reliability.	👎 Asking people about a hypothetical situation is an issue of ecological validity. They may behave differently in real life.

Now try this

Kaz is dating Al but fears he is unfaithful. She confides in her friend, 'If it were just sex, I could handle it, but I'm afraid he's in love with her.'

Use your knowledge of Buss et al.'s study to explain why Kaz is more worried about Al falling in love than having sex with someone else.

Use Buss et al.'s findings to explain the behaviour in the scenario. Kaz is female so you must refer to what Buss found out about female reactions to types of infidelity.

The Deady et al. study (2006)

Key study 'Maternal personality and reproductive ambition in women is associated with salivary testosterone levels' is a study from the **biological approach** that looks at how an aspect of a woman's physiology (a hormone level) influences her maternal behaviour.

Key principles

This study used a questionnaire method to gather self-reporting data and a physical measure of testosterone, in order to establish the degree of relationship between the two. The **aim** was to investigate the relationship between maternal and reproductive drive in women, and the amount of testosterone in their saliva.

Procedure

1 British female undergraduate students completed the Bem Sex Role Inventory (BSRI) in order to establish a measure of their maternal characteristics. There were also questions about future maternal ambitions.

2 Samples of saliva were taken from each woman in order to analyse the level of testosterone.

3 These two measures were correlated.

Findings

1 Participants with the highest levels of salivary testosterone were least likely to express strong positive feelings about children and becoming a mother.

2 The higher the level of testosterone, the longer the participant intended to wait before having a child.

Conclusion

These findings suggest that having a high level of the masculine hormone testosterone impacts on maternal drive in women. The presence of the hormone affects potential behaviour.

Real world Explaining behaviour

The application of this study is socially sensitive as it suggests that men, with their high levels of testosterone, would not be good carers of small children. This is demonstrably not the case, as some men take on the main caregiving role. Testosterone cannot be the only factor in the development of gender roles.

Evaluating strengths and limitations of the study

Strengths	Limitations
👍 The measures used in this study were reliable and valid. The BSRI is an established measure of gender that has recognised validity.	👎 The measure of maternal ambition lacked validity because it asked the participant to speculate about an unknown future. Attitudes could change over time.
👍 The study was well controlled throughout. For example, the measure of testosterone level in saliva was objective and scientifically verified.	👎 The study cannot prove a causal relationship; it merely shows a link. We do not know if high testosterone affects maternal ambition or whether maternal ambition affects testosterone.

Now try this

Explain the findings of Deady et al.'s study into maternal ambition.

 When explaining findings, you will need to include conclusions.

The Harlow study (1868)

📖 **Key study** 'Passage of an iron rod through the head – the case study of Phineas Gage' is a study from the **biological approach** by Harlow. It presented a case study of brain damage as an insight into the neuroanatomy of the brain. By linking a loss of function to the site of damage, it is possible to infer that function is situated in that location in the brain.

Key principles

This is a case study of a single subject – Phineas Gage, a railway foreman – who suffered serious head trauma when an iron rod was blasted up through his left eye and out of the top-left side of his head. He survived and his recovery was documented. Unusually, there were no real **aims**; Harlow simply followed what happened to Phineas Gage during his recovery and sent his findings to a journal, which published the account.

Procedure

There was no procedure, other than to document Gage's day-to-day progress as he recovered.

Findings

1 Gage lost most of his left frontal lobe.

2 Anecdotal accounts suggested that his behaviour changed: having been controlled and self-disciplined, he became childish and impulsive, frequently refusing to follow doctors' advice and often becoming irritable.

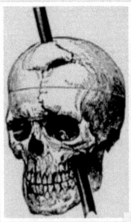 

Phineas Gage survived an iron rod being blasted through his head. Harlow documented the effect on Gage's behaviour.

Conclusions

From this case, it seems that the left frontal lobe has a function in controlling emotions, personality and behaviour, and in decision-making.

🌐 **Real world** **Explaining behaviour**

Cases like Gage's have useful application in mapping brain structure to behavioural function, which is helpful in the understanding and treatment of brain injury.

Evaluating strengths and limitations of the study

Strengths	Limitations
👍 Case studies like this tend to have high ecological validity as they simply track what happens to real people in the real world.	👎 The issue with this case study is lack of detail – there is no official record of the extent of the brain injury or of Gage's behaviour before the injury.
👍 It is possible to collect and record in-depth data when studying a single individual.	👎 Single case studies lack population validity. It may be that Gage was in some way unusual and that other people with the same injury would have responded differently.

Now try this

Assess the use of case studies in investigating the role of biology in behaviour. Refer to the case of Phineas Gage in your answer.

This question is asking you to weigh up the use of case studies, with particular reference to biological psychology and Phineas Gage.

Cognitive approach to aggression

Psychological concepts and research can be used to explain contemporary issues of **aggression in society**. There are different types of aggression including **hostile** and **instrumental**. The **cognitive approach** includes **priming** for aggression and **hostile attribution bias** (HAB) (see pages 4–5). It proposes that how the mind processes information is a fundamental influence on behaviour. To understand people's reactions, you need to understand the beliefs that underpin behaviour.

Aggression in society

Aggression is an issue of relevance to society. Aggression can be:

- **instrumental** – deliberate and designed to achieve an aim
- **hostile** – reactive and angry, with the intention of causing harm.

Real world Recent statistics show a rise in the number of violent crimes. Many of these crimes are the result of aggression, especially hostile aggression.

Application of the cognitive approach

The cognitive approach can be used to explain aggression in many contexts. Psychologists can explain why some people are more aggressive than others by looking at how they:

- use their **beliefs** to interpret what is going on around them
- **process information** from the environment using biases and schema.

Role of scripts and schema

People organise their knowledge of the world in a set of interconnected schema that develop over time and with experience.

- If someone has a lot of experience of aggression, their **schema** will be biased towards aggression.
- People with aggressive schema may have **cognitive scripts** that lead them to aggressive outcomes.

Real world Violent cognitive scripts may be learned from exposure to violent media, such as video games.

Priming for aggression

Cues in the environment can trigger schema that contain cognitive scripts for aggression.

A picture of a gun might prime for an aggressive reaction if the individual has developed schema based on gun violence in a video game.

Hostile attribution bias (HAB)

Some people are more likely to interpret signals from others as hostile.

- They do not use rational thinking to process all the information available to them.
- They automatically see aggressive intent in other people and react with aggression.

Real world Someone with HAB might interpret an accidental touch as threatening and react angrily.

Application of cognitive research to aggression

Research shows that people convicted of violent crimes are much more likely than non-violent criminals to assume that photos of ambiguous facial expressions are hostile. Such people have HAB which might explain their convictions.

Now try this

Fina grew up with domestic violence.

Using concepts drawn from the cognitive approach, explain why, as an adult, she may react to her own domestic disagreements with inappropriate violence.

 This is an explain question so you must make sure that you have provided a reason for your answer.

Social approach to aggression

The **social approach** to explaining **aggression in society** includes **conforming to social and group norms**, and **stereotypes**. The social approach proposes that people are influenced by their social context and that this affects their behaviour (see pages 9–10). You can understand why people react the way they do if you understand social influences.

Application of the social approach

Hostile and instrumental aggression can be defined as aggressive behaviour that is calculated to achieve a goal or personal gain. It can be explained within the context of social situations. People's behaviour is influenced by:

- **group norms** – how a social group normally behaves
- **stereotypes** – their beliefs about the characteristics of their own and other groups.

Conformity to norms

Conformity is a powerful social influence.

- People tend to base their attitudes and behaviours, including relating to aggression, on that of social groups.
- If group members accept and use aggression, new recruits to the group are likely to adopt similar attitudes.

Normative social influence

Once part of a group that has norms in which aggression is acceptable, an individual might comply in order to fit in. They may not actually think that aggression is a useful response, but will go along with it.

Real world If someone joins a gang with a norm for carrying and using knives, they might also carry a knife and threaten others with it. Privately, they may not want to. They become aggressive purely in order to fit in with the group.

Informational social influence

This type of social influence results in a stronger conformity. If the group is an important part of a person's identity and the group leaders have reasons for aggression (alleged oppression), through **internalisation** the person is likely to change behaviour in a way that is both private and public, and is long-lasting.

Real world If gang leaders say that society is responsible for their problems, a new member may truly accept the norms of the gang. They may willingly carry a knife and use it to assert the gang's views.

Stereotyping

A stereotype is a belief about members of a social group. Stereotyping can lead to aggression against members of the stereotyped group especially if the stereotype:

- dehumanises the other group
- suggests that the other group is hostile.

Aggression and the social studies

Haney et al. (1973) showed that people could behave aggressively, even if out of character, when they felt it was expected of their social role (see page 13).

Meeting members of a rival gang can activate stereotypes that opposing gang members are dangerous and hateful. People might behave aggressively before any threat has been made.

Now try this

Following the London riots of 2011, many people were prosecuted for fighting, arson and looting. Social media was said to have influenced the anti-social behaviour of young people.

Explain why some young people might have been socially influenced to behave in this way. Use knowledge of conformity in your answer.

Use normative and informational social influence to explain why some people went along with group behaviour.

Learning approach to aggression

The **learning approach** to explaining **aggression in society** suggests that behaviour is learned through the consequences of **interacting with the environment** and by **observing others** (see pages 14–15). You can explain why people act aggressively if you consider that they may have **learned** the behaviour.

Application of the learning approach

The learning approach proposes that behaviour is a product of both direct and indirect experience of the environment.

- **Direct learning** – individuals are **conditioned** to give an aggressive response.
- **Indirect learning** – people learn to be aggressive by observing aggression in others.

Operant conditioning

This is learning through the consequences of behaviour (see page 15).

- Aggression is learned if it is positively or negatively **reinforced**.
- Aggression will not be learned if the behaviour is **punished** rather than rewarded.

Reinforcement of aggression

In operant conditioning, behaviour – in this case aggression – is learned by consequences. If it is punished then we learn not to be aggressive, but if it is reinforced we learn to be aggressive.

Positive reinforcement

Aggressive acts that lead to an instant reward are positively reinforced. This means that the person is likely to be aggressive again in the future. They have learned that aggression leads to rewards.

 If a child gets into a fight at school and other children cheer and admire their behaviour, their social status rises. This is a positive consequence so the child is likely to be aggressive in future.

Negative reinforcement

Aggressive acts that lead to the avoidance of punishment are negatively reinforced. They are likely to be repeated because avoiding a punishment is a good thing.

 If a child is picked on by another child, this makes them feel bad. They may hit the other child to make them stop. If then they are no longer picked on (negative reinforcement), in similar future situations they may also show aggression.

Social learning

Aggression can be learned by observation.

- If we see other people behaving aggressively, and we identify with them, we may **model** our behaviour on theirs, especially if they were not punished or were rewarded for their aggression (**vicarious reinforcement**).
- In this way, we learn that aggression is an appropriate and useful response.

Aggression and the learning studies

Bandura (1961) showed that children learned aggressive play behaviour through social learning by watching adults play aggressively.

If a child sees a popular peer being admired for fighting, they are likely to imitate the role model.

Now try this

A footballer is harassed and insulted by the crowd. He responds by slamming the ball into the crowd and is sent off.

Explain whether the footballer is likely to repeat this behaviour, using your knowledge of operant conditioning.

You can revise operant conditioning on page 15.

27

Biological approach to aggression

The **biological approach** to explaining **aggression in society** suggests that behaviours are inherited through **genes** and depend on **neurobiology** (see pages 20–21). Biology explains why some people are more aggressive than others.

Application of the biological approach

The biological approach explains aggression as a product of **nature** rather than **nurture**. People are born with innate traits, which include aggression, as a result of genetic inheritance (nature).

Genes

Aggression can be transmitted through the generations in our genes (see page 20).

- If we have parents who are aggressive, we are more likely to be aggressive too.
- Scientists have isolated some genes that are strongly associated with aggression, such as the warrior gene. People with a particular form of this gene are more likely to show aggression than those with a different form.

Evolution

Aggression is a behaviour that has evolved due to selective advantage (see page 21).

- In the environment of evolutionary adaptation, aggression increased survival of human males.
- It made them better providers. They could hunt animals and protect their mates and resources.
- Females were more likely to select these successful males as mates.

Brain structures

Brain structures are involved in behaviour.

- The limbic system processes emotions.
- The prefrontal cortex controls impulsive behaviour.
- Abnormalities in the limbic system and prefrontal cortex can lead to aggression.
- These brain abnormalities can be genetic or from brain damage from trauma or abuse.

Neurochemistry

Aggressive behaviour is linked to:

- abnormally high or low levels of some neurotransmitters or hormones
- a high testosterone level, which is associated with competitiveness and aggression in some people. Aggression is more likely in males than females, possibly due to testosterone levels.

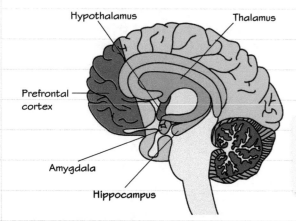

Limbic system

Hypothalamus   Thalamus

Prefrontal cortex

Amygdala

Hippocampus

Application of biological research to aggression

Research on a prison population found that males who were convicted of violent offences had higher salivary levels of testosterone than those who committed property crime.

> If someone has an abnormally small amygdala (part of the limbic system), they are more likely to interpret situations around them as hostile and react with violence.

Now try this

Terry has been convicted several times of grievous bodily harm. He cannot control his temper and says his brother and dad are the same.

Explain why Terry might be right in saying that he cannot control his aggression. Use concepts drawn from the biological approach in your answer.

> It is possible to argue that Terry is aggressive because of social learning or hostile attribution bias, but the question focuses on the **biological approach**. As the scenario mentions Terry's father and brother, genetics is the best answer.

Cognitive approach to business

Psychology can be used in **business** to explain and influence consumer behaviour, including **types of advertising** (product recognition and campaigns aimed at changing public opinion). Psychological concepts and research from the **cognitive approach** can be used to understand and inform strategies that aim to **change behaviour** in business settings.

Influencing consumer behaviour

Cognitive psychology focuses on how information processing influences thinking and behavioural change. It is used in business to influence buying decisions, for example through advertising and product packaging.

Cognitive priming in advertising

Advertising often uses priming (see page 4).

- **Repetition priming** – the product and the brand name are often paired, so the product automatically triggers the name.
- **Associative priming** – the product is regularly associated with something else, so one triggers the other.

 • The mention of 'baked beans' triggers a familiar brand name.

- Green-coloured packaging is associated with environmental responsibility.

Scripts and schema

Priming works by activating schema that contain information which is relevant to the situation. This affects how people react to products and situations.

 The use of music can activate schema. For example, happy music triggers positive schema which can influence buying behaviour.

Subliminal messages and brainwashing in advertising

- In **subliminal messaging**, a change is triggered in consumers at a subconscious level, for example by a favourable impression of a product.
- **Brainwashing-style** techniques, such as repetition, can alter consumers' thinking and decisions without them being aware of it. Flashing images viewed subconsciously is illegal in many countries.

Biases in information processing

Biases are mental shortcuts that increase the speed of information processing, so we make fast decisions based on learned patterns (see page 5).

 Most people value products based on price, and can be manipulated to choose a product on that basis. They are most likely to choose a product that is neither the most nor least expensive.

Cognitive approach studies and business psychology

Harris et al. (2009) demonstrated how it is possible to trigger schema in people and so change their behaviour through showing advertisements (see page 7). This has direct relevance for the use of advertising to change consumer behaviour.

Now try this

A psychology teacher serves red lemonade and asks learners to identify the flavour. Most say cherry. However, if they are blindfolded, they know it is normal lemonade.

Explain why the learners mistake the drink's flavour when they can see the colour. Use concepts from cognitive psychology in your answer.

The answer must link to cognitive concepts, so consider which are the most appropriate before you answer the question. It is an 'explain' question so you must give a reason for your answer.

Social approach to business

Psychological concepts and research from the **social approach** can be used to understand and inform strategies that aim to **change behaviour** in business situations, through conformity to social norms.

Influencing consumer behaviour

People often make decisions about their consumer behaviour based on the behaviour of others. By providing information about what others do in similar situations, it is possible to influence how people behave.

 People can be influenced by advertising to:

- buy a product or donate to charity
- adopt a healthier lifestyle
- recycle.

Conformity to social norms

Social influence works by convincing people that others within their social groups behave in a specific way. To be in line with group norms, individuals change their behaviour to be the same as the group.

This works through **two** ways:

1 normative social influence

2 informational social influence.

1 Normative social influence

People change behaviour to fit in with a social group out of fear of being excluded. This is the **bandwagon effect**, whereby we do what the group does to be part of it.

- In order to be accepted by a group, people might buy a particular product.
- Advertisers can convince us that a product is popular within the group.

 iPhone users identify as a specific group. In order to support that identity, they always use an iPhone.

2 Informational social influence

People change behaviour from a belief that the group has knowledge that we don't. This is the **social proof effect**.

- In terms of consumer behaviour, people buy products that are popular.
- This is because they assume the group has persuasive information about the product.
- They are likely to buy the product in order to appear similarly informed.

 Use of persuasive statistics such as 'Nine out of ten people recommend our product' is a common advertising tactic.

Other applications

Social media uses conformity pressures to encourage participation.

 If someone has lots of followers on Twitter, we are encouraged to follow them because others must have a good reason for following them. This is an example of social proof influencing behaviour.

Application of social research to business

Psychologists found that hotel guests who were shown a message that said the majority of guests reuse their towels were 26 per cent more likely to reuse them than guests shown a standard message about the value to the environment of towel reuse.

Now try this

Some people think that graphic displays of voter reactions (real-time worm line graphs) should be banned on televised debates during election campaigns in case they influence viewers.

1 Identify which kind of social influence would be most likely to affect viewers of these programmes.

2 Justify your answer.

This is a two-part question. First, a simple answer naming the type of social influence is required. Then you have to explain why you think this is correct, so you must relate your answer to the information in the scenario.

Learning approach to business

Psychological concepts and research from the **learning approach** can be used to understand and inform strategies that aim to **change behaviour** in business situations using advertising, public health campaigns and other social initiatives. The learning approach suggests that behaviour is influenced by interaction with the environment and that by altering aspects of the environment behaviour can be changed (see pages 14–16).

Changing behaviour in business

The learning approach is used to influence consumer decisions through the use of:

- role models, such as in health promotion campaigns (social learning)
- the association of events (classical conditioning) such as in retail situations
- reinforcement of desired behaviour (operant conditioning), such as in supermarket loyalty point cards.

Social learning theory

Social learning theory proposes that people:

- learn by observing others' behaviour
- imitate behaviour if it is modelled by someone they identify with and are motivated to follow
- change their behaviour when exposed to **role models** who demonstrate and are reinforced for showing specific behaviour.

Real world Celebrities often feature in advertising campaigns. If an admired celebrity is using a product, you may imitate them.

Classical conditioning

Classical conditioning involves learning by the association of stimuli with responses. This can create **two** potential responses.

1 **Aversion** – for example, anti-smoking strategies involve creating associations between cigarettes and disgusting images of bad teeth or diseased lungs. The aim is to cause the smoker to feel disgust when they see a cigarette.

2 **Desire** – used in advertising by associating positive feel-good images and music with products, so the product makes the consumer feel good.

Smoking causes mouth and throat cancer

Get help to stop smoking at www.nhs.uk/quit

Here **classical conditioning** is being used to create an aversion to the stimulus. The **UCS** is the photo of mouth cancer. The **UCR** is disgust. The cigarettes (**NS**) become associated with the picture of the mouth. Cigarettes are the **CS** when they cause disgust (**CR**).

Operant conditioning

Operant conditioning occurs when a person learns from the consequences of their own behaviour. Behaviour that is **reinforced** is likely to be repeated.

Real world Many supermarkets and shops reward customers with points to encourage loyalty and repeat purchases.

Operant conditioning and social media

Many people find the responses they get for posting on social media reinforcing. When they post and get a 'like' it makes them feel good, so they post more to get more likes. This is **positive reinforcement**. Failing to get likes is aversive, so people keep using social media. This is **negative reinforcement**.

Now try this

Top football player Eden Hazard has been endorsed by sports brand Nike.

Explain why Nike would choose Hazard to advertise their product.

 This is an 'explain' question, which means you have to give a reason and then justify what you say.

Biological approach to business

Psychological concepts and research from the **biological approach** can be used to understand and inform strategies that aim to **change behaviour** in business situations through neuromarketing – scanning techniques to detect brain change in consumer decision-making.

Understanding consumer behaviour

As technology advances, it is possible to observe the inner workings of the brain, which can be more accurate than asking people what they think or feel.

Biological psychologists use technology to understand the physical changes in the brain that are associated with positive and negative responses to products and advertising.

Biological influences on decision-making

Investigation techniques include:

- **eye-tracking**, which is used to measure the direction and duration of gaze
- **electroencephalography (EEG)**, which measures changes in electrical activity across the brain
- **functional magnetic resonance imaging** (fMRI), which measures oxygen uptake in the brain (indicating activity in specific locations).

Neuromarketing

Neuromarketing is about gathering research into consumer buying habits using psychology and neuroscience. It focuses on what triggers buying habits, such as stimuli. It uses biological techniques to:

- understand what makes adverts effective
- manipulate product and packaging design in order to appeal to the unconscious processes that influence our buying decisions.

 Real world Using eye-tracking technology it is possible to determine which features of an advert or product gain the most attention. In this way, attention-grabbing elements are used most effectively.

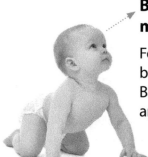

Babysoft for the most sensitive skin

Formulated for your baby's delicate skin, Babysoft is soothing and natural.

Eye-tracking technology has demonstrated that adult gaze is attracted by images of babies and what babies are looking at, so effective adverts show the baby looking at the message.

Localisation of function

Research has led to a map of brain function, including identification of those areas that are associated with a positive emotional response to a product or advert. This means it is possible to judge which advert or product design is most appealing before launching it.

Biological approach research

Recent research in the USA using fMRI scanners found that it was possible to predict whether or not someone would buy a product based on activity in the reward centres of the brain and in the prefrontal cortex.

 Now try this

Discuss the use of biological concepts and research techniques to influence consumer behaviour.

The command word 'discuss' tells you this is an extended open response question. You must describe the use of biopsychology, for example neuromarketing, and explore the subject using reasoned arguments to develop your answer.

Cognitive approach to gender

Psychological concepts and research can be used to understand and explain **typical** and **atypical gender** of individuals in society. The influence of the **cognitive approach** on gender involves the role of **biases** and **schema** (gender schema theory).

Gender

Gender is the psychological characteristics of masculinity or femininity experienced by an individual.

- Traditionally, this has been seen as a **binary** situation whereby an individual is either masculine or feminine.
- More recently, society has recognised that this model is too simplistic, as many people do not identify as either gender or choose a gender that does not match their biological sex.

Using psychological terminology

Here are some explanations of terminology used in relation to gender. Terminology relating to gender may change over time.

Masculinity – characteristics that are traditionally associated with being male.

Femininity – characteristics traditionally associated with being female.

Non-binary – a gender choice that is neither masculine nor feminine.

Gender-fluid – the experience of not having a fixed gender.

Androgyny – gender that has characteristics associated with both masculinity and femininity.

Transgender – the experience of switching gender towards that of the opposite sex.

Gender dysphoria – distress caused by a mismatch between biological sex and psychological gender.

Typical and atypical gender

- In **typical** gender, biological sex matches gender, so females have feminine characteristics and males have male characteristics.
- In **atypical** gender, individuals do not display the characteristics associated with their biological sex.

Applying the cognitive approach

The cognitive approach explains gender as a product of **information processing**. Our **beliefs** about gender influence how we feel about our own and others' gender, and this affects our **gendered behaviour**.

Role of biases in gender

Confirmation bias reinforces the schema that we hold about gender. We tend to:

- disregard or distort information that is inconsistent with our beliefs about gender-appropriate behaviour
- recall information which is consistent with our beliefs about gender.

 Real world Research shows that when young boys see a male in an atypical gender role, such as a nurse, they may not recall it or will change the man's identity to doctor or paramedic.

Role of gender schema theory

Young children build schema about gender which become more complex with age and experience.

- Initially, children have simple gender schema centred on in-group ('same as me') and out-group ('not like me').
- They pay more attention to those in their in-group and base their behaviour on their standards and attitudes.
- Based on their in-group, they build their understanding of their own gender.
- This gives them a rich schema for same-sex behaviour that influences how they behave.

 Now try this

Define what is meant by the term **gender dysphoria**.

This is a simple recall question which does not need explanation or examples.

Social approach to gender

The influence of the **social approach** on gender involves **peer influences** (normative and informational) and **conformity** to gender roles.

Applying the social approach

The social approach to gender focuses on how other people influence our behaviour. It would argue that gendered behaviour is a product of social situations and reflects the attitudes of others in our social groups.

Real world A young girl might watch other girls playing gender-specific playground games and believe that, to fit in with the girl group, she must play these games (normative social influence). She then plays the same games in order to be correct (informational social influence).

Conformity to gender roles

Our behaviour is influenced by the social groups we belong to.

- Gender is a social group.
- **Social norms** for gender apply within the group.
- **Informational social influence** and **normative social influence** cause people to conform to those norms.

Peer pressure

Normative social influence impacts on gender behaviour.

- People conform to the gender behaviour of the gender group they belong to in order to fit in and be liked.
- Peer pressure causes people to engage in behaviour that is acceptable to the group.

Real world A young boy might agree with other boys if they express gender stereotypes about suitable male behaviour.

Stereotypes

Stereotypes reflect the **gender norms** held by society and they affect how people interact.

- Typical gender stereotypes have centred on masculinity as male identity and femininity as female identity.
- Some stereotypes can be negative.

Real world Boys who display behaviour associated with female identity might be negatively labelled. This stereotype affects how they are treated in social interactions.

Changing trends in gender

Norms and stereotypes change over time.

- The majority view of acceptable gender behaviour has shifted in society.
- Typical gender stereotypes are breaking down and more people feel able to choose a non-traditional gender.
- Informational social influence has an effect as people learn more about alternative genders. A range of atypical gender is developing as a result.

Androgynous models such as Casey Legler, a female menswear model, challenge attitudes about typical gender and provide new norms for young people.

Now try this

Trainee teachers Eimear and Stephen are on playground duty. Eimear expresses surprise at how physical the boys are compared to the girls. Stephen says, 'Boys will be boys'.

Explain Stephen's response, using concepts you have learned from the social approach.

This question asks for you to explain typical male gendered behaviour through the use of stereotypes. In an 'explain' question, you must back up what you say with a reason.

Learning approach to gender

The **learning approach** to gender involves **conditioning** and **social learning**.

Applying the learning approach

The learning approach proposes that behaviour is learned directly or indirectly from the environment. In this approach, typical and atypical gender is learned through conditioning or through observation.

 People in society are exposed to a wide range of gender models. Some transgender people such as Caitlyn Jenner have high-profile celebrity careers, and their gender choices are reinforced by media attention.

Conditioning

Operant conditioning is direct learning. The person experiences positive or negative reinforcement or punishment for a behaviour and repeats or stops it. In this way, people build up a set of behaviours that reflect their gender.

 If a boy cries when called a rude name, his friends may tease him. Teasing is punishing, so he will try not to cry again. Alternatively, if he punches the name-caller, his friends may cheer and reinforce him. In this way, he learns a typical gender identity for a boy (aggression, not emotion).

Social learning

Social learning is indirect learning. We tend to:

- observe and remember the behaviour of those with whom we identify, such as same-sex role models
- replicate the behaviour of role models, if we are able, especially if they were reinforced for their action.

 A younger boy seeing an older one respond aggressively to teasing and then being cheered by others for doing so is more likely to imitate the aggression because it was reinforced.

Conditioning and changes

Changes in gender can be explained through conditioning. As ideas about gender-appropriate behaviour change, people's responses to 'atypical' gender behaviour are also changing.

- People may no longer experience punishment for atypical gender behaviour.
- A less restrictive set of learned behaviours is considered appropriate for all genders.

 A boy who cries might experience sympathy rather than ridicule.

Social learning and changes

Changes in gender can be explained through social learning. As gender becomes less rigid, people are exposed to role models with atypical genders. Younger people are likely to imitate high status models rather than traditional ones, breaking down rigid and traditional ideas of gender.

 We often see males modelling typically female behaviour, such as stay-at-home dads, and female politicians modelling traditionally male behaviour.

Learning approach studies

Learning approach studies relevant to gender, for example Bandura (1961), showed children learn behaviours by observing adults and learn more from same-sex role models.

Now try this

Tia puts lipstick all over her face. Her mum laughs and says she is 'just like mummy'.

Explain why Tia is likely to repeat this behaviour, but her brother Joe is unlikely to use lipstick in this way. Refer to concepts from the learning approach.

 This question has many possible answers. Think about how you will answer the parts about Tia and Joe. You may need to use different reasons for each child.

Biological approach to gender

The influence of the **biological approach** on gender involves the role of sex hormones (before and after birth) and evolutionary explanations for masculinity and femininity.

Applying the biological approach to gender

Biological sex is assigned at birth as male or female based on observable physical characteristics. Gender is the psychological feelings of masculinity or femininity.

- In **typical** gender development, biological sex matches gender.
- In **atypical** gender development, the individual identifies as different from their biological sex.

Role of sex hormones in females

1. Foetus inherits X chromosomes from both parents.
2. Lack of Y chromosome sets default pathway for foetus to develop as female.
3. Low testosterone means brain develops as female; female genitals and sex organs develop.
4. Secondary sexual characteristics develop at puberty.

Role of sex hormones in males

1. Foetus inherits X chromosome from mother and Y from father.
2. Y chromosome carries masculine genes, which trigger release of testosterone in foetus.
3. Testosterone causes development of male genitalia and masculinises the brain.
4. Male sex organs release more testosterone at puberty, reinforcing masculinity of the brain.

Evolutionary explanations for masculinity and femininity

For a species to be successful, males and females must mate, conceive offspring and raise them to maturity. In the environment of evolutionary adaptation:

- Successful adult human females were mostly pregnant and rearing children. Risky behaviours such as hunting were not adaptive as these would threaten their child-rearing abilities.
- Successful males evolved in size and strength to provide resources and protection for females.

- Genetic differences that led males to show more masculine behaviour were **selected** by females to ensure their offspring had the best chance of survival through access to their father's resources.
- Males selected females who were genetically likely to be successful mothers.

Explaining atypical gender development

The biological approach suggests that, just as typical gender development results from physical factors such as genes, brain structure and chemistry, atypical development results from changes in these aspects.

Real world An area of the brain called the sexually dimorphic nucleus has been found to vary in those who are transgendered.

The biological approach studies

- Buss et al. (1992) demonstrated differences in men's and women's attitudes to sexual fidelity (page 22). The findings may support the evolution of gendered characteristics.
- Deady et al. (2006) showed that a higher testosterone level in women was associated with a reduced maternal drive (page 23).

Now try this

Although assigned as a boy at birth, Andi has always chosen to identify and live as a female.

Explain Andi's experience of atypical gender, using your knowledge of biological concepts.

This is an 'explain' question, so identify a suitable concept and give a clear reason for your choice.

Your Unit 1 exam

Your Unit 1 exam will be set by Pearson and could cover any of the essential content in the unit. You can revise the unit content in this Revision Guide. This skills section is designed to **revise skills** that might be needed in your exam. The section uses selected content and outcomes to provide examples of ways of applying your skills.

Exam checklist

Before your exam, make sure you have:

- ✓ a black pen you like and at least one spare
- ✓ double checked the time and date of your exam
- ✓ a good night's sleep
- ✓ eaten in a healthy way
- ✓ water.

Check the Pearson website

The questions and sample response extracts in this section are provided to help you to revise content and skills. Ask your tutor or check the Pearson website for the most up-to-date **Sample Assessment Material (SAM)** and **Mark Scheme** to get an indication of the structure of your actual paper and what this requires of you. The details of the actual exam may change so always make sure you are up to date.

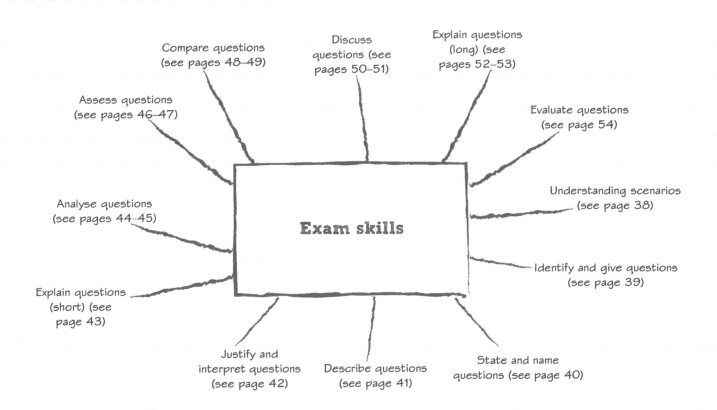

Compare questions (see pages 48–49)

Discuss questions (see pages 50–51)

Explain questions (long) (see pages 52–53)

Assess questions (see pages 46–47)

Evaluate questions (see page 54)

Analyse questions (see pages 44–45)

Understanding scenarios (see page 38)

Exam skills

Identify and give questions (see page 39)

Explain questions (short) (see page 43)

Justify and interpret questions (see page 42)

Describe questions (see page 41)

State and name questions (see page 40)

Now try this

Visit the Pearson website and find the page containing the course materials for BTEC National Applied Psychology. Look at the latest Unit 1 SAM for an indication of:

- the paper you have to take
- whether the paper is in sections
- how much time is allowed and how many marks are allocated
- what types of questions appear on the paper.

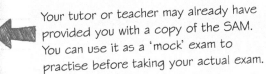

Your tutor or teacher may already have provided you with a copy of the SAM. You can use it as a 'mock' exam to practise before taking your actual exam.

Understanding scenarios

Some questions start with a scenario that gives a real-life context for the question.

Relating to vocational contexts

Scenarios use **realistic situations** and **vocational contexts** to test your understanding of how psychology can be applied to explain behaviour.

✓ Scenarios can relate to one question.

✓ Scenarios can develop over a series of questions so you find out more information. You are asked different questions at different stages as the scenario develops.

✓ Read a scenario carefully so that you can select appropriate concepts to apply to it.

✓ Select information from the scenario to link to your application of psychology.

Applying approaches and concepts

When asked to apply your learning about psychological approaches to behaviour:

✓ the question may specify which approach and/or concept to use to explain the behaviour, or you may need to select the appropriate approach yourself

✓ the scenario will mostly focus on aggression, gender or business behaviour

✓ you could be asked more than one question on a scenario because the same behaviour can be explained using different psychological concepts.

Worked example

1 Asha always shops at the same supermarket, even though it is further from her house than another shop. Her friend AJ suggests she would save time by shopping closer to home. Asha refuses, saying she gets loyalty points at her supermarket, which she can exchange for special offers over the year.

Explain Asha's shopping behaviour using concepts drawn from the learning approach.

Asha is being operantly conditioned to shop at the same place. The supermarket is positively reinforcing her behaviour by giving her points that she can swap for something she wants.

2 AJ challenges Asha's views and suggests she is being brainwashed by the supermarket. Describe what is meant by brainwashing.

Brainwashing is a term that describes how events in the environment influence the process of making a decision without the person being consciously aware of it.

3 Explain AJ's statement that Asha has been brainwashed by the supermarket.

Asha automatically goes to the same shop without thinking because she has been conditioned by the brand to shop only there.

 The question asks you to explain behaviour and specifies the learning approach. Consider what the characters in the scenario are doing. There are three theories: classical conditioning, operant conditioning and social learning. The best choice here is operant conditioning.

 The relevant concept is identified and then explained using effective terminology such as 'positive reinforcement'.

 This develops the previous scenario and is a simple question asking you to define a term.

 This is a comprehensive answer that mentions the role of the environment and the fact that the person is unaware of the influence.

 The question is asking you to link the concepts described earlier to the example of brainwashing.

Although brief, this clearly answers the question without repeating information. It links well to the concepts described earlier and explains how the supermarket manipulates Asha by conditioning her.

Now try this

The manufacturers of a remote-controlled toy car want children to ask for the toy for Christmas. World champion Formula One racing driver Lewis Hamilton will appear in the advertising campaign.

Explain why Lewis Hamilton is an appropriate choice for this product. Use your knowledge of the learning approach.

 **Links** To revise social learning theory, see page 16.

Identify and give questions

If you are asked **identify** or **give** questions, they require short answers without development. Demonstrate your psychological knowledge and recall key assumptions, concepts and research. Make sure your answer is appropriate and uses the correct terminology.

Worked example

Ben eats at a fish restaurant but contracts a stomach bug at the same time so is very sick. Now the smell of fish is enough to make him nauseous. His friend tells him this is because of classical conditioning where an unconditioned stimulus that causes an unconditioned response is associated with a neutral stimulus until that stimulus becomes a conditioned stimulus because it produces the same response.

Identify the unconditioned stimulus in this scenario.

The stomach bug.

This scenario clearly links to classical conditioning. The question requires you to select the thing that causes the response naturally and without learning.

When you identify, you do not need to justify your answer. Here, the conditioned stimulus is identified, using words from the scenario.

Identify the conditioned stimulus in this scenario.

The smell of fish.

This question requires you to select from the scenario the thing that Ben has learned to produce the response to.

Using the words of the scenario, identify the right element.

Conditioning is a concept that is relevant to the learning approach.

Give **one** key assumption of the learning approach.

Behaviour is a product of direct learning from the environment.

This is a recall question. Briefly give a key assumption that is appropriate for the stated approach. You should know all key assumptions for each approach.

Social learning theory is an example of indirect learning from the environment.

Give **one** reason why social learning is indirect learning.

It is indirect because it involves learning by observing what happens to others, rather than having to experience something first.

A 'give a reason why' question includes a statement and the only requirement is to give the reason why. Here, the answer is comprehensive and clearly gives an appropriate reason why social learning is indirect.

Now try this

Teachers of young children often use star charts to encourage good behaviour. Children who behave well get a star, and when they get enough stars they choose a reward such as a treat. This is an example of operant conditioning.

1 Give **one** reason why the use of star charts is a form of operant conditioning.

2 Identify an example of positive reinforcement in this scenario.

1 The question states that it gives an example of operant conditioning, so the reason you give needs to justify it.

2 To identify an example, find the part of the description that represents positive reinforcement.

Links To revise operant conditioning, see page 15.

State and name questions

If you are asked **state** or **name** questions, they require short answers with no development. Demonstrate your psychological knowledge and recall key assumptions, concepts and research. Your answer should be clear, using specialist terms.

Worked example

Loftus and Palmer (1974) studied the effect of leading questions on recall of a car accident. The study tested how the wording of a question about the speed at which the cars were travelling at impact influenced the answer.

State **one** finding from this study.

When the word 'smashed' was used in the question, participants recalled the speed of the cars as being higher.

The question is based on a key study. You must know about each key study in Unit 1. Here, you need to recall from memory facts about the research. No further detail is needed.

There are other findings but it is enough to say that the highest speed was recalled when the word 'smashed' was in the question.

Reconstructive memory theory claims that our memories are constructed at the point of recall and change over time in predictable ways. One way they change is through rationalisation.

State **one** other way this theory says that memory is changed.

Shortening is another way memory changes.

The question is based on an outline of a key psychological concept from the cognitive approach. Based on the example of rationalisation given in the question, you need to recall one other way memory is changed.

The answer could also be shortening or confabulation.

Name **one** type of priming.

Associative priming.

With a 'name' question, use the correct terminology as you recall a correct term or concept, as required by the question.

Name **one** level of conformity.

Compliance.

This question calls on knowledge of the key concepts of the social approach. Other answers could be 'identification' or 'internalisation'.

Now try this

According to the social approach, people conform to the behaviour of social groups due to conformity. This is a form of social influence.

Name **one** form of social influence.

This points you towards the social approach and specifies social influence. There are two types of social influence. Name one of them.

Links To revise social conformity, see page 9.

Describe questions

If you are asked a **describe** question, you need to give an account of something. Develop the statements in your response as they are often linked, but there is no need to include a justification or reason. You may be asked to describe concepts, approaches, research and applications. Read the question carefully so you understand what it is asking for in your answer.

Worked example

Biological psychologists study how the brain works. They sometimes use case studies of brain damage.

Describe **one** study from the biological approach that investigated the effect of brain damage on behaviour.

Harlow's (1868) study of Phineas Gage investigated the brain damage suffered by Gage when he accidentally blew a metal rod through his head. Harlow documented his recovery and recorded what happened to him. Before the accident Gage was well mannered and responsible, but after the accident he was more impulsive and less able to control himself. His friends said his personality had altered. As his frontal cortex was damaged, it can be concluded that this area of the brain is responsible for personality and impulse control.

This brief statement prompts you to think about studies from the biological approach and sets a context for the question. The question directs you to the Harlow study of Phineas Gage, the only relevant study from the biological approach.

You need the skills to construct a coherent answer, with good terminology based on knowledge. The amount of detail needed depends on how many marks are offered. This is a fairly comprehensive answer with a clear statement about behavioural change and a conclusion about the role of a specific brain area.

Michael is aged 24 and has just been convicted of assault and grievous bodily harm. This is his third conviction for violence against the person. The judge is considering imposing a prison sentence on him. Michael's lawyer argues that the judge should take into account when sentencing that Michael's aggressive behaviour is beyond his control. The lawyer states that Michael's father has a similar record for violence and is currently serving a life sentence for murder.

Describe concepts from the biological approach that could be used to support the lawyer's argument.

The concept of genetic inheritance could be used to support the lawyer's argument. Aggression such as that displayed by Michael could be genetically programmed with genes inherited from his father. They may both possess genes that make them vulnerable to becoming violent.

This scenario focuses on aggression and the reasons why someone is habitually aggressive. The clues are that this is Michael's third conviction and his father has a similar history. The question is asking you to state facts about an application of psychology.

This is a detailed account. It focuses on one biological concept and clearly links it to the scenario.

Now try this

Describe **one** way that cognitive psychology can be applied to consumer behaviour.

Links To revise the cognitive approach to business, see page 29.

Justify and interpret questions

If you are asked to **interpret**, you need to recognise a trend or pattern within a given scenario. If asked to **justify**, you need to give reasons or evidence to support a statement in the question. You must demonstrate your understanding of the link between psychological assumptions, concepts and research to behaviour in society.

Worked example

Research by Williams (1981) tracked the behaviour of children in three towns in Canada. One town already received several TV channels, the second received one TV channel but was given more channels, and the other previously had no TV but received some channels for the first time. They found that the children in the no-TV town that were given TV showed a big increase in aggressive behaviour.

Interpret these results using social learning theory.

The children in the no-TV town had no exposure to programmes with characters behaving aggressively and then suddenly high exposure to aggressive characters. The children might identify with these models and imitate their behaviour. The increase in exposure to aggressive models through the introduction of TV would explain the increase in the children's aggression.

Interpretation is an important skill for researchers, to help them understand findings. Here, the question asks you recognise a pattern in the data, but also to link the pattern to a specific theory.

The answer first identifies the trend (increase in TV channels). It then takes the main principles of social learning theory of observation modelling and imitation, and links to the outcome of increased aggression based on TV viewing.

Vicky runs her office tea fund. People should put money in an honesty box to cover the costs of their hot drinks. Vicky noticed that the sum raised was less than £10 per month, so she put up a notice reminding people to pay. In that month £11 was raised. She then tried putting a picture of eyes above the drinks station and found that workers contributed £17.

Interpret the change in contributions to the tea fund.

The amount contributed to the tea fund rose when people were reminded to contribute but only by a small amount. However, when they thought they were being watched by the eyes, there was a much bigger increase.

This is a real-world situation where psychological principles have been used effectively. It shows how subconscious priming affects behaviour. The question asks you to look for trends in the scenario.

You could work out percentages to demonstrate change, but it is enough simply to show how the contributions increased over time and to link this to cognitive concepts.

Vicky told others about what happened and claimed that cognitive priming had changed behaviour.

Justify Vicky's claim.

Vicky thinks the eyes subconsciously primed the staff to think they were being watched, which made them more likely to contribute honestly to the fund.

This statement follows on from the above scenario with a further question. Notice that Vicky's claim is that cognitive priming had occurred. The answer justifies Vicky's statement by linking the behaviour in the scenario to the concept of priming.

Now try this

Consider Skinner's research into operant conditioning and link your answer to the statement.

Skinner (1932) claimed that the consequences of an act affect the probability of it occurring again.

Justify this statement using your knowledge of operant conditioning.

Links To revise the Skinner study, see page 19. To revise operant conditioning, see page 15.

Explain questions (short)

If you are asked an **explain** question, you need to justify and exemplify your points, giving reasons. Demonstrate your understanding by explaining the link between psychological assumptions, concepts and research and behaviour in society.

Answering explain questions

Explain questions can require **shorter** or **longer** answers. An example of a longer answer is given on pages 52–53. Below are some examples of shorter answers.

When answering this kind of question:

☑ identify a point, and then justify or exemplify the point you have made to show your knowledge and understanding

☑ link your answer to the context given in the question

☑ make sure your answer is clear, using the correct terminology.

Worked example

Deady et al. (2006) found that the amount of testosterone in the saliva of women was related to their maternal ambitions.

Explain how testosterone is linked to maternal behaviour.

Maternal ambition is a feminine behaviour. Testosterone, a hormone, is linked to masculine behaviour, so high levels of testosterone would lead women to feel less maternal.

 This gives a brief account of the findings of a key study. The question requires you to consider a concept drawn from the biological approach.

 When you explain, you need to identify a point and then justify or exemplify it. Here, the use of the word 'so' links the point with the reason given for the behaviour specified in the question.

Debra's son Adam is running around 'shooting' his friend with a stick. Debra says it is because she let him watch a film with a gun fight between police and criminals.

Explain Debra's belief, using your knowledge of concepts drawn from the learning approach.

Debra is referring to social learning theory. Adam has seen shooting behaviour modelled on TV. He has identified with the models and is imitating their behaviour as best he can, so he pretends to shoot his friend.

 This gives a brief outline of real-world behaviour. The question requires use of concepts from the learning approach. Here, the explanation needs to be linked to why Adam is playing at shooting.

 The answer identifies the most appropriate concept from the learning approach and shows how it can be applied to the scenario. The language used is accurate and appropriate.

Now try this

Explain how Bandura et al.'s 1961 study of the transmission of aggression through observation supports the claims of social learning theory.

 This requires knowledge of the findings of Bandura et al's study to explain how they support the ideas of social learning theory. Focus on the explanation of the difference between children who witnessed aggression and those who did not, and apply key terms appropriately from social learning.

 Links To revise the Bandura et al. study (1961), see page 17.

Analyse questions

If you are asked an **analyse** question, you need to present the outcome of a **methodical** and **detailed** examination.

Answering an analyse question

You might need to:

✓ break down a **themed topic** or **situation** in order to interpret or study the **relationship between the parts** (for example, to show the relationship between the unconditioned stimulus and response in classical conditioning)

✓ break down **information** or **data** to interpret and study **key trends** or **interrelationships** (for example, to show how theories or concepts can be used to explain changes in society, such as increasing cases of atypical gender).

Qualities in your answer

Consider how your response to an analyse question will:

✓ show accurate and detailed knowledge and understanding

✓ break the situation down into component parts, making points that are relevant to the context in the question

✓ display a well-developed and logical analysis that clearly considers interrelationships or linkages in a sustained manner

✓ select the most appropriate theory or concept to demonstrate your understanding.

Worked example

The Swedish government has actively discouraged the use of gender stereotyping in the education system. Starting at kindergarten level, teachers are encouraged to ensure that boys and girls get the same opportunities and are not treated differently because of their gender.

Analyse the effect of stereotyping on gender development.

In your answer you should consider:

- social categorisation
- stereotyping.

You may be given a brief scenario when asked an analyse question. Make sure the points you make are relevant to the context in the scenario and the question. This question focuses on gender. The analysis skill required would be the same with any content and section of the exam.

For longer answer questions, you could make a brief plan to structure your answer and note key materials you will use. For example, Chatard et al.'s key study would be relevant when responding to this question.

Sample response extract

Gender is a basic social category which is imposed on children through their lives by stereotyping. From birth, children are separated into males and females. Categorisation into groups leads to the application of stereotypes where members of the group are assumed to have qualities associated with the group. For example, boys are assumed to be more physical in their play than girls, who are assumed to be more nurturing.

This extract from a response starts by selecting the right material from the social approach. You need to show accurate and detailed knowledge of social categorisation and stereotyping, and apply it to gender.

The answer continues on the next page.

Analyse questions (continued)

The example **analyse question** starts on page 44 and continues below.

Stereotyping based on gender can affect children's gender development as they conform to fit in with other's expectations. Some theorists have referred to this as a 'gender straitjacket' because the children have no choice but to assume the stereotypical behaviour expected of them.

Make sure you consider both points in the question. Break the situation down into parts, showing how things link together. In this case, social categorisation leads to stereotyping which leads to conformity. Develop your points in your analysis. Here, the answer develops to analyse social concepts associated with gender development. A logical analysis is given, that clearly considers how stereotyping affects gender development.

This might have a serious impact in secondary education where boys and girls select different subjects and are taught different things. For example, girls would be much less likely to study engineering than boys. This limits the life chances of both genders.

Develop your points further in a sustained way. Here, the analysis is taken to a logical outcome relevant to the context of education.

In Sweden teachers are trained to avoid stereotypes such as telling little boys that boys don't cry and encouraging little girls to play with dolls. This will stop children being limited by the gender stereotypes associated with being male and female, and give them genuine choices in their future careers because they believe they can do anything.

Make sure that you refer to the stimulus material in the question. Having analysed the potential effect of stereotypes, here the response goes on to explain why the Swedish government is trying to reduce them.

Chatard et al. (2007) showed that stereotypes affect how people think about themselves when they found that girls recalled their maths exam scores as lower than they were, when they were reminded of the stereotype that girls are not as good at maths as boys.

You could use a key study in your conclusion. Relate it back to the question rather than just describing the results. Here, the analysis of the importance of stereotypes is concluded by using the findings of a key study. This supports the argument that gender stereotyping impacts on gender development, which has consequences for the person.

Now try this

Make notes that outline an answer for the following question:

Analyse the role of social learning theory in the development of a person's gender.

In your answer you should consider:

- the role of models in the process
- observational learning.

Here, the focus is still on gender but the question asks for a different theory.

 Links To revise social learning theory, see page 16. To revise gender, see pages 34 and 35.

Assess questions

If you are asked an **assess** question, you need to give careful consideration to varied factors or events that apply to a specific situation and identify which are the most important or relevant. Make a judgement on the importance of something and come to a conclusion.

Answering assess questions

If answering an assess question that includes a scenario and requires a longer answer, such as the example below, consider how you will:

☑ apply psychology to a specific topic

☑ relate your answer to the scenario

☑ select and provide appropriate material

☑ demonstrate your knowledge and understanding of relevant psychological concepts

☑ consider alternative or competing explanations

☑ develop your answer to show potential outcomes.

Worked example

A local council has received complaints from residents living close to a small shopping centre that young people are hanging around in the evening, making noise and behaving anti-socially. One resident suggests they install a 'mosquito device' which emits a high-pitched sound that only young people can hear and which they find unpleasant.

Assess the possible impact of this intervention on the behaviour of the young people.

In your answer you should consider:

• operant conditioning

• classical conditioning.

You may be given a brief scenario when asked an assess question. Make sure the points you make are relevant to the context in the scenario and to the question.

This question focuses on the learning approach, specifically conditioning. The 'assess' skills required would be the same with any content and section of the exam. Here, the question is asking for an assessment of which factors are the most important and what effect they may have.

Sample response extract

Conditioning involves learning by direct experience of the environment. Classical conditioning is learning through associations between events, whereas operant conditioning involves learning through the consequences of our own actions.

This extract from a response opens by providing a brief and accurate account of both theories of conditioning.

In this context, classical conditioning would explain the use of the device. The sound it makes is an unconditioned stimulus, causing an unpleasant reaction in the young people who can hear it. The place where they heard it is initially a neutral stimulus, but will be associated with the noise and become a conditioned stimulus causing the conditioned response of unpleasant reaction, so the young people will no longer want to go to that place. In this way, the device will successfully cause the young people not to hang round the shopping centre.

Make sure you link your assessment to the context of the question and use key terms effectively. Here, the answer applies classical conditioning to the scenario and uses key terms appropriately. It links to the potential impact of the device in order to assess the situation.

The answer continues on the next page.

Assess questions (continued)

The example **assess question** starts on page 46 and continues below.

Similarly, operant conditioning will cause the young people to move away through negative reinforcement. If they leave the area, they will feel better because they avoid the unpleasant noise, so they are reinforced for finding somewhere else to hang out.
This means they will avoid the shopping centre in future.

While the use of the device is likely to be successful in moving the young people away from the centre, it will not stop them from being noisy. All they have learned is that the shopping centre is not a good place for them. Also, other local young people who are not involved in the noise will suffer from the device and cannot move away. This is not ethical.

Make sure you consider both points in the question. Here, the answer moves on and applies operant conditioning to the scenario, using effective terminology.

You need to make a judgement and come to a conclusion in your answers to 'assess' questions. Here, the overall success is considered by looking at the costs and benefits of the device.

Using a brief plan

If an assess question requires a longer answer:

☑ use your skills in assessing the value of psychological research

☑ avoid unnecessary description

☑ you could make a brief plan to keep focused on the requirements of the question.

Example plan

The plan below relates to the example answer above. It shows a logical development and is clearly focused on the scenario and on conditioning.

* Briefly outline conditioning.
* Link to the scenario – use classical conditioning UCS noise > UCR unpleasant feeling > NS shopping centre.
* Assess effect on behaviour of young people.
* Operant conditioning – negative reinforcement causes young people to learn to go somewhere else.
* Conclusion – assess wider impact of using this technique.

Now try this

Make a brief plan to answer the following question.

It is claimed that aggression runs in families, suggesting a genetic link.

Assess the claim that aggressive behaviour is a product of our biological make-up.

In your answer you should consider the role of:
* hormones
* evolution.

Your plan for this answer will be different from the example above.

* The focus is less specific and calls for you to assess the biological approach.
* The question gives some indication, for example, genetics.
* You could assess the claim by bringing in alternative explanations that may form better arguments.

 To revise the biological explanation for aggression in society, see page 28.

Compare questions

If you are asked a **compare** (or **compare and contrast**) question, you need to look for similarities and differences in two or more things. Your answer should relate to all features mentioned in the question, and must include at least one similarity and one difference. No conclusion is required.

Answering compare questions

Compare questions may require longer answers. Consider how you will:

- ✓ show good subject knowledge and application to the scenario
- ✓ identify and explain points of **difference** between concepts, explanations or research
- ✓ identify and explain points of **similarity** between concepts, explanations or research
- ✓ provide clear links between the competing explanations on points of difference and similarity
- ✓ display effective use of key psychological terminology.

Worked example

Typical and atypical gender can be explained in multiple ways. Some would argue that gender is a product of nature over nurture.

Compare and contrast the biological explanation for gender with that of the learning approach.

In your answer you should consider:
- the key assumptions of each approach
- both typical and atypical genders.

You may be given a statement or scenario as a context for a compare question. Ensure that the points you make are relevant to the context and the question.

This question focuses on gender. The comparison skills required would be the same with any content and section of the exam.

Sample response extract

The biological approach claims that gender is a product of nature and is innate, resulting from biological differences between the sexes. In contrast, the learning approach proposes that gender is learned through direct or indirect experience of the environment.

Those following the biological approach would argue that typical genders, in which males feel masculine and females feel feminine, stem from evolutionary pressures. For example, masculine men were more successful in the environment of evolutionary adaptation because they made better providers, and successful women were those who were nurturing.

This extract from a response starts by outlining the broad claims related to what is being compared and links them to the focus of the question. In this case, the focus is gender. Notice that terms such as 'in contrast' or 'on the other hand' can be used to clearly signal a comparison.

Develop your answer with more detail, using key terminology. Here, the focus is on typical gender development. More detail is provided using key terminology, such as 'the environment of evolutionary adaptation'.

The answer continues on the next page.

Compare questions (continued)

The example **compare question** starts on page 48 and continues below.

On the other hand, those following the learning approach would explain typical gender through the application of operant conditioning. For example, young boys' behaviour is reinforced for showing stereotypically masculine behaviour and girls for showing feminine behaviour. In this way, they learn to be the gender they are, showing how nurture may be influential.

An appropriate comparison is sustained, as shown here, so when choosing points to compare, make sure you can argue for both theories. Avoid inappropriate comparisons, for example claiming that one theory focuses on nurture but another theory has a lot of evidence.

The biological approach investigates gendered behaviour through physical means, such as looking for differences between male and female brains using scanning techniques, or through measuring differences in biochemistry such as testosterone levels. The learning approach investigates gender through observations of differences in the behaviour of males and females, such as watching to see which toys boys and girls will play with.

Most approaches use different methodological techniques to investigate their claims. This can provide a point of difference in the comparison.

Both approaches suggest that gender is not a matter of choice. They suggest we are programmed by nature or by nurture to become masculine, feminine or gender-fluid by events we do not control.

It is important to find a similarity between the explanations for gender. A similarity such as this would apply across many explanations for gender.

Using a brief plan

It can be useful to make a brief plan to keep focused on the requirements of a longer question. For the above question, for example, an answer plan might be:

- nature vs nurture (innate, biological vs direct or indirect experiences)
- evolutionary pressures to masculinity/femininity vs cultural and social modelling and experience
- similar – both can explain atypical gender development, although in different ways
- different – each approach employs different methods to explore gender.

Now try this

Plan an answer for this similar question.

Compare and contrast the biological explanation for aggression with an explanation from the learning approach.

You need to identify suitable comparison points, but the plan could be similar to the one above for the question on gender.

In your answer you should consider:
- key concepts from the biological approach
- key concepts from the learning approach
- explanations for aggression.

Links To revise the learning approach to aggression in society, see page 27, and for the biological approach, see page 28.

Discuss questions

If you are asked a **discuss** question, you need to identify the issue, situation, problem or argument that is being assessed in the question. You should explore all the aspects and investigate them by reasoning or argument. A conclusion is not required.

Qualities in your answer

Consider how your response to 'discuss' questions will:

✓ show accurate and detailed knowledge and understanding

✓ be relevant and link to the context in the question

✓ display a well-developed and logical discussion which clearly considers a range of different aspects and how they link together, to produce a coherent answer to the question.

Worked example

Businesses are increasingly using psychological techniques and ideas in order to change consumer behaviour.

Discuss the use of psychological concepts in business.

In your answer you should consider concepts from:

- the biological approach
- the cognitive approach.

You may be given a brief statement or scenario when asked a discuss question. Make sure the points you make are relevant and applied to both the context given and the question.

The question focuses on the application of psychology to consumer behaviour. The discussion skills required would be the same with any content and section of the exam. Make sure that you cover the key terms in the question.

Sample response extract

Businesses use psychology in order to manipulate consumers into buying products. They do this by designing advertising campaigns and product packaging that are memorable and appealing to the consumer. Biological psychology is used to gauge physiological responses to different adverts, while cognitive psychology uses priming techniques to influence what we pay attention to and remember about products.

This extract from a response starts by showing accurate knowledge of the ways psychology is used in relation to the question – here, to change consumer behaviour. Provide more detail as you develop an answer. Here, the paragraph becomes more specific by naming ways in which psychology is used.

Biological psychology involves the use of techniques that detect changes in brain activity and direction of eye movement in order to assess whether a particular product package or advert has an impact on the viewer. For example, EEG machines detect increased activity in certain brain areas, which can then be linked to whether those areas are activated when the person experiences liking for the product or advert. This is called neuromarketing, and some might argue that spying on the workings of the brain in order to sell goods is not a good use of psychology.

Focus on one approach and apply detail as to how it is used to influence consumers, using the correct terminology. Discuss a range of aspects related to the question. Do not only describe them. For example, here there is some evaluation of the use of neuromarketing.

The answer continues on the next page.

Discuss questions (continued)

The example **discuss** question starts on page 50 and continues below.

Cognitive psychology is applied to marketing through priming, which involves activating schema that are favourable to the product. For example, using upbeat and happy music when displaying the product triggers a happy schema. The good feeling becomes associated with the product. So when the product is available in the shop it is primed by association to cause you to feel happy, so you are more likely to buy it.

Make sure you consider both points in the question. For example, here there is a change to discuss the other approach. The discussion develops in a logical way with a clear explanation, using effective terminology drawn from the approach, of how it can change consumer behaviour.

Using relevant examples in a discussion is an effective way of illustrating the points and linking them to the context in the question.

There is research evidence that shows how priming affects consumer behaviour. Harris, Bargh and Brownell (2009) found that exposing children to adverts for food while watching a cartoon increased the amount of food they ate. This shows how schema can be activated by priming and how this schema then changes how individuals feel and behave. In this case, it activated an eating schema and the children ate more. This suggests that priming does really change behaviour.

Use research evidence to back up the claims in your discussion. Make sure you show how the results could apply to the question. Here, research evidence is given for priming and how it changes behaviour in a way that can be applied to consumers.

Focus on the question

If answering a longer 'discuss' question:

- ☑ keep focused on the question
- ☑ show knowledge and understanding through the selection of the most appropriate concepts in order to answer the question
- ☑ demonstrate breadth of knowledge by discussing differing or competing theories that can be applied to the question
- ☑ do not waste time on irrelevant information that does not directly answer the question.

Make a brief plan

You could make a brief plan to keep your answer focused. Here is a sample plan for the 'discuss' answer above.

- Outline role of psychology in consumer behaviour – brief link to advertising/ packaging.
- Explain why these techniques are used.
- Describe a biological technique that is used – neuromarketing/eye-tracking.
- Briefly evaluate the use of this method.
- Describe a cognitive technique – priming activates schema, such as happy music.
- Briefly evaluate method – Harris study supports role of priming to change behaviour.

Now try this

Write a brief plan for the following question.

Discuss how the learning approach is used to influence consumer behaviour.

In your answer you should consider:

- social learning theory
- operant conditioning.

This question has just one approach but with three key concepts: social learning theory, operant conditioning and classical conditioning. Here, two have been selected as the focus of the question.

Links To revise how the learning approach is used in business, see page 31.

Explain questions (long)

If you are asked an **explain** question, you need to justify and exemplify the points that you explain, giving reasons. In your answers, apply and evaluate psychological assumptions, concepts and research to explain contemporary issues of relevance to society.

Answering explain questions

Explain questions can require **longer** or **shorter** answers. Examples of short answer questions are given on page 43. Here is an example of a longer answer. When answering these kinds of questions, consider how you will:

Ⓥ look for ways in which the question guides you to what psychological approach to use

Ⓥ make sure that you give reasons for what you say

Ⓥ develop your answer so that you have thoroughly justified your explanation.

Worked example

Local politicians are worried about a rise in crimes of violence among young people. They believe that gang culture is to blame.

Explain how aggression could be linked to gang culture.

In your answer you should consider:

- normative and informational social influence
- social learning theory.

 You may be given a brief statement or scenario when asked an explain question. Make sure the points you make are relevant to the context and to the question.

 The question focuses on aggression and how it can be explained by concepts from the social approach and the learning approach. The explanation skills required would be the same with any content and section of the exam.

Sample response extract

Social influence suggests that we change our behaviour to conform to that of others around us. When young people join a gang, they accept the norms of the gang and conform to those norms. This might be due to normative social influence, where they do what the other gang members do in order to fit in and be part of the group.

It may be because of informational social influence: they believe that the other gang members know the right way to behave, so they conform to the gang norms in order to be in the right.

If the gang has norms that include violence then the members of the gang will conform and commit violence in the 'right' circumstances, for example if confronted by members of an opposing gang.

 This extract from a response links explanation to the behaviour in the question. Here, the answer starts with the social approach, outlining what social influence is and including the different types, relating it to the behaviour in question.

Keep your answers focused on the question. Here, the answer links directly to gangs as it continues.

 Keep your explanation clear. Using examples can help link your explanation to the context of the question. Here, the explanation links to the question by using the concepts to relate violence to gang membership.

The answer continues on the next page.

Explain questions (long) (continued)

The example **explain (long answer)** question starts on page 52 and continues below.

If a young person joins a gang and the people with higher status in the gang commit violence, the young person learns this is the right thing to do. The older gang member is a model with whom the young person identifies. Their actions are imitated by the young person, especially if they are reinforced.

Make sure you cover both points you have been asked to consider in the question, including relevant key terms. Here, the answer makes a switch to social learning and goes on to include several key terms such as imitation, reinforcement and identification.

For example, if the older gang member is respected by other gang members for fighting – if they are not caught and punished – then the younger members will learn that the way to resolve issues is through violence. This is because violence was vicariously reinforced and is easy to imitate.

Continue to focus on the context and question. Here, the explanation is clearly linked to gangs and violence.

In this way, increase in violence among young people can be explained through applying social learning theory and social influence to gang culture.

The explanation ends clearly, linking back to the question and context.

Using a brief plan

If answering a longer 'explain' question, you could make a brief plan to keep the focus on the context and question, and to ensure that they are linked. For the above question, for example, an answer plan might be:

- Outline social influence – normative and informational.
- Explain how each concept explains aggression in gang members through conformity.
- Outline social learning theory, including key concepts of modelling, imitation and reinforcement.
- Explain how social learning could lead to aggression within a gang.

Now try this

Make a brief plan for an answer to this similar question.

Explain how concepts from the cognitive approach to psychology would account for aggression.

In your answer you should consider:

- hostile attribution bias
- priming.

  To revise the cognitive approach and aggression, see page 25.

Evaluate questions

If you are asked an **evaluate** question, you need to consider various aspects of a subject's qualities in relation to its context, such as strengths or weaknesses, advantages or disadvantages, pros or cons. You need to come to a judgement, supported by evidence, often in the form of a conclusion.

Answering evaluate questions

If asked an 'evaluate' question, the length of your answer will depend on the marks available. Here is an example of evaluation skills within a longer answer. Make sure that you focus on **evaluating** what you are asked about, and **limit** any description.

Worked example

Phineas Gage features in a well-known case study in psychology which shows how damage to a specific part of the brain can affect personality and behaviour.

Evaluate the case study of Phineas Gage.

In your answer you should consider

- strengths of the study
- limitations of the study.

You may be given a brief statement or scenario when asked an evaluate question. Make sure the points you make are relevant to the context and to the question.

This question focuses on a key study. The evaluation skills required would be the same with any content and section of the exam.

Sample response extract

The case study of Phineas Gage by Harlow (1868) had high ecological validity as it occurred in real life and was not part of an experiment. Gage's injury was caused by a genuine accident and his recovery was recorded as it happened.

It would be unethical to deliberately damage a person's brain in order to establish the function of the damaged part, so using case studies like that of Gage is a good way to map functions to specific brain areas.

However, Gage was a single participant and he may be unrepresentative of the general population. His brain might have responded differently to the accident than others and his recovery may not have been typical. We cannot generalise from single cases like Gage's, limiting their usefulness.

A further problem was in the way the case was documented. The doctor in charge wrote it as a letter rather than as scientific document, so the level of detail was not sufficient to be able to draw valid conclusions.

On balance, although the study has some validity, it is limited in its usefulness because it lacks reliability.

Start by briefly planning your answer to an evaluate question. Think about strengths and limitations of the study – a good start is to link the study to ecological validity.

Make sure you develop your evaluation. Here, the evaluation develops by considering a further strength.

Consider both strengths and limitations. Here, the evaluation switches to a limitation. As this is a case study, a key issue is one of generalisation.

Continue to develop your answer to a conclusion. Here, a further limitation is evaluated – that the study was not written up using a scientific format. Be sure to say why this is a problem.

Finish your answer with a brief but appropriate conclusion.

Now try this

Bandura et al. (1961) concluded that children learn behaviour by observing the actions of models.

Evaluate Bandura et al's. 1961 study on the transmission of aggression through imitation of aggressive models.

Links To revise the Bandura et al. study (1961), see page 17.

Health and ill health

Key aspects of health and ill health can be identified and defined using **biomedical**, **biopsychosocial** and **health continuum models**.

Biomedical model

The biomedical model focuses purely on **biological** aspects of health and suggests that:

- a person is healthy in the absence of disease

- ill health is due to abnormalities in the body that cause specific **physical** symptoms (e.g. from genes, bacteria, viruses and chemicals)

- scientific measures define states of health and illness in a **medical** model practised by doctors and health professionals with the emphasis on diagnosis (through x-rays, scans and blood tests) and treatments (through vaccinations, medication, surgery and hospitalisation).

Real world Lung cancer caused by smoking can be diagnosed via X-ray and treated by surgery and medication.

Biopsychosocial model

The biopsychosocial model is a development of the biomedical model that integrates other factors. It is a **holistic** (whole-person) approach that considers lifestyle and the effect on health of the interaction between:

- **physical/medical/biological aspects** – genes, bacteria and viruses, for example

- **psychological aspects** – health beliefs such as attitude to pain; mental health issues such as stress; and behaviours such as coping mechanisms

- **social aspects** – class, employment and ethnicity, for example.

Real world A person ill from stress might receive cognitive behavioural therapy (psychological aspect) that involves joining a sports club and making friends (social aspect), which reduces their insomnia (a biological response).

Health as a continuum

The health continuum is a type of scale from very good health to very poor health. It recognises that:

- physical/medical/biological, psychological and social aspects impact on health at all stages and places them on a **continuum**

- the **combination** of different factors influence where an individual is along the health continuum

- individuals can change their behaviour to improve their health along different aspects of the continuum.

Real world
- For **psychological wellbeing**, an individual could use health-coping strategies such as yoga or meditation to reduce stress and move along the continuum.

- An individual with a **chronic health condition**, with mobility and personal care needs, might improve their health by understanding their health needs, taking medication, sleeping and eating well, exercising where possible and taking part in social activities.

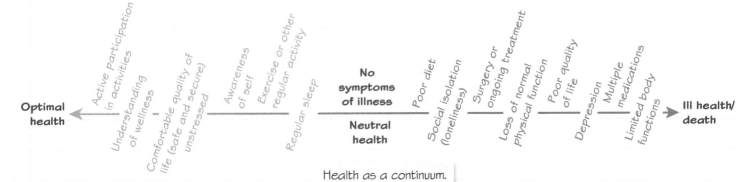

Health as a continuum.

Now try this

Compare the biomedical and biopsychosocial models with the model of health as a continuum.

Be sure to compare all three models, drawing out the similarities and differences.

55

Behavioural and physiological addiction

Addiction is the **physiological** (biological) or **behavioural** (psychological) overdependence on a substance, such as nicotine or alcohol, or psychological overdependence on a behaviour, such as working, gambling or shopping.

Definitions

Behavioural addiction is a psychological compulsion to engage in behaviour despite a negative impact on an individual's daily life.

Physiological addiction is when an individual experiences physical symptoms from using or **withdrawing** from a substance.

Explaining behavioural addiction

This addiction is learned through interaction with the environment and other people in **three** main ways.

1 In **classical conditioning**, exposure to an environmental stimulus can become associated with substance use, so that the environment can stimulate cravings.

 If someone used to smoke when drinking alcohol, they may find that the taste of beer triggers nicotine cravings.

2 The concept of **operant conditioning** suggests that addiction is positively reinforced by acceptance in social situations where other people use the same substance.

 Drinking with friends positively reinforces alcohol's physical effects.

3 **Social learning theory** suggests that observing role models who receive positive reinforcement for their behaviour influences addiction in others.

 If a teenager observes an admired peer smoking, they may decide to try it.

Explaining physiological addiction

Physiological addiction has biological causes in **two** main ways.

1 **Addictive substances** alter brain chemistry, either by imitating the brain's own chemical messages or by interfering with the brain's reward pathway.

 Cocaine and heroin are addictive substances. They both affect the normal transmission of nerve messages and stimulate the brain's reward pathway.

2 **Biological predisposition**, through inheritance of genes, can make some people more vulnerable to addiction.

 Addictive tendencies can run in families due to inheritance of genes.

Characteristics of behavioural addiction

People with shopping and gambling addictions commonly experience:
- issues with impulse control
- denial of the addiction
- feelings of sadness or depression when engaging in the behaviour or shortly after
- a need to conceal the behaviour from friends and family.

Characteristics of physiological addiction

People who use addictive chemicals such as nicotine and alcohol may experience:
- cravings for the drug
- physical **withdrawal** symptoms, such as sweating, and psychological symptoms, such as anxiety, if they do not take the drug
- **tolerance** – the need to take more and more of the drug to get the same effects.

Now try this

Explain the difference between behavioural addiction and physiological addiction.

 Make sure that you cover both types of addiction. Use an example of each to help illustrate your answer.

Griffiths' components of addiction

Griffiths' model (1996) describes **six characteristics (components) of addiction** that can be applied to real-life examples.

① Physical and psychological dependence (salience)

For this component of addiction, salience means that addiction is the most important thing in the person's life.

- In **psychological dependence**, the addict focuses completely on the addictive drug or behaviour so that it dominates their existence and they neglect other aspects of their life.

 A shopping addict thinks about shopping and the next purchase all the time, and may ignore family commitments.

- In **physical dependence**, the chemical influences physiology, such as the dopamine reward system, and the addict's body adapts to the drug.

② Tolerance

Increasing amounts of the addictive substance or engagement in the addictive activity are required to obtain the same physical, psychological or emotional responses.

 A heroin addict has to take larger and larger doses of the drug in order to get the same experience (euphoria).

③ Withdrawal

An individual may experience unpleasant feelings or physical effects when they stop engaging in the activity or consuming the substance.

 Physiological withdrawal effects could be sweating, feeling sick and headache. **Psychological** effects could be irritability and moodiness.

Withdrawal symptoms can cause people with an addiction to relapse.

④ Relapse

In addiction there is a tendency to repeat previous behaviours, which are quickly restored after a period of abstinence.

 A smoker who gave up smoking for several years can return to the addictive behaviour after smoking a single cigarette.

⑤ Conflict

- **Interpersonal conflict** between the addict and those around them is common.
- **Intrapsychic conflict** may also exist **within** the individual, if they understand the consequences of their addictive behaviour but feel unable to stop.

 Some addicts have no contact with their families.

⑥ Mood alteration

These are the experiences that the individual may report when engaging in the addictive activity.

 Playing online games increases arousal, which may be addictive.

Describe how an alcoholic's behaviour could be explained, using Griffiths' six-component model of addiction.

You should demonstrate understanding of all six aspects of the model in the context of alcohol addiction.

Stress

The term **stress** applies to the body's **psychological responses** (effects on thinking) and **physiological responses** (effects on the body) to a situation or event.

Defining stress

Stress can be defined by key characteristics.

- It occurs when an individual is presented with a demanding set of circumstances.
- It is experienced differently by individuals as everyone has a different level of **ability to cope**.
- It can be **positive** if it drives someone towards a goal, or **negative** if it causes psychological or physical distress.

Psychological impacts of stress

Psychological stress occurs when an individual can no longer cope with the stressor. Psychological effects of stress can be:

- **cognitive** (to do with thinking), such as worry, restlessness, negativity or shame
- **emotional** (affective), such as moodiness, sadness or anger
- **perceptual** (related to a person's attitude), such as despair at feeling unable to cope.

Stressors

A stressor can be a situation, event or pressure that triggers a response in an individual.

- A **situation** might be starting a new job.
- A bereavement is an **event**.
- The need to gain a specific grade in an examination is a **pressure**.

Perceived ability to cope

The effects of stress occur when a person encounters a stressor that exceeds their perceived ability to cope.

- A perceived ability to cope is someone's personal assessment of how well they can manage a stressor.
- **Coping skills** are the methods an individual employs to reduce the effects of the stressor, such as to remove themselves from the stressful situation.

 Real world If someone finds their job very stressful, they may look for a new one.

Physiological impacts of stress

Acute (short-term) stress has immediate physical effects on the body.

Chronic (long-term) stress causes health issues.

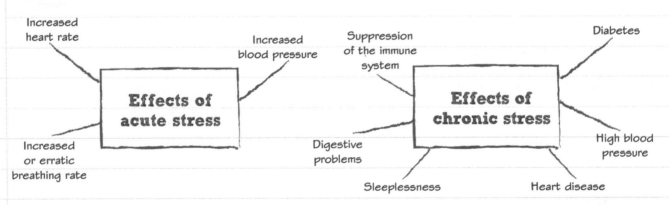

Increased heart rate — Effects of acute stress — Increased blood pressure

Increased or erratic breathing rate

Suppression of the immune system — Effects of chronic stress — Diabetes

Digestive problems — Sleeplessness — Heart disease — High blood pressure

Now try this

What is stress?

This question is asking you to give a definition.

Rosenstock's health belief model

 Key theory **Rosenstock's health belief model theory** (1966) is a psychological model that explains and predicts health behaviours.

Key features

The health belief model (HBM) is from the **cognitive approach**. It considers factors that affect health decisions and behaviour. It is one way that psychologists attempt to predict whether people will be successful in overcoming addiction. It can be applied, for example, to smoking, alcohol, gambling and shopping.

Perceived seriousness/severity

Perceived susceptibility

Factors that affect health decision-making

Perceived barriers

Perceived benefits

① Perceived seriousness/severity

The probability that an individual will change their behaviour depends on how **severe** the consequences are considered to be.

 Real world The seriousness of lung cancer might cause a smoker to give up.

③ Perceived benefits

People consider the costs and benefits of making health changes (cost–benefit analysis).

* **Benefits** – changing behaviour has positive outcomes.
* **Costs** – disadvantages of behavioural change that prevent people from acting.

 Real world A person is more likely to stop smoking if it **benefits** them, such as being able to save money. Irritability is a **cost** of quitting.

② Perceived susceptibility

Individuals will not change their behaviour unless they feel they are at risk.

Real world People who think their risk of getting lung cancer from smoking is low are unlikely to stop smoking.

④ Perceived barriers

People assess factors that support or discourage the behaviour. Barriers to making health-related decisions may be **financial**, **situational** or **social**.

Real world The **cost** of nicotine replacement therapy can be a barrier. In stressful **situations**, smoking may provide relief of stress. If everyone else in a person's peer group smokes, they may feel **socially** excluded if they try to give up.

Demographic variables

There are individual differences in how people take health-related decisions, connected to demographic factors such as age, gender, culture, education level or personality.

 Real world If an individual gains a detailed understanding of anatomy and physiology through their **education**, they may decide to give up smoking.

Cues

Cues or triggers are reminders that the person needs to change their behaviour.

* **External** cues are outside the person.
* **Internal** cues occur in the mind or body.

Real world Health warnings on cigarette packets are **external** cues to give up. A feeling of breathlessness could be an **internal** cue to stop smoking.

Now try this

Marie's GP says she is at risk of liver damage and stroke due to her alcohol consumption. Marie makes these statements: 'My chance of getting liver cancer is very low,' and 'My grandad had a stroke but recovered.'

Identify which of the statements is an example of perceived seriousness and which is a perceived susceptibility.

An **identify** question is asking you to select the correct answer from information given in the scenario.

The Becker et al. study (1978)

Key study Many people don't follow medical advice. Becker et al.'s study, '**Compliance with a medical regimen for asthma**' examines adherence using the **health belief model** (HBM) (see page 59).

Key principles of Becker et al. (1978)

Aim and procedure

Compliance with medical advice is low in chronic conditions such as asthma.

- The **aim** was to use the HBM to explain mothers' adherence to asthma treatment for their children.
- In the **procedure**, mothers were interviewed about their children's health and asthma treatment. Blood samples were used to measure compliance with asthma treatment. Mothers were allowed to withdraw participation at any time.

Findings

1 **Positive correlation** was found between mothers' beliefs about the **seriousness** of asthma and compliance with treatment, and between beliefs about **susceptibility** to an attack and adherence.

2 Mothers who thought that the **costs** (disadvantages) of asthma attacks included disruption of schooling and of their own activities were more compliant.

3 **Barriers** were: scheduling treatment, disruption of normal activities, difficulties accessing prescriptions, taste of the medicine.

4 Being married and educated (**demographic variables**) were associated with compliance.

Conclusions

All of the major HBM components were good predictors of health-related behaviour.

👍 The findings support Becker et al.'s **assumption** that the four components of the HBM, demographic variables, internal cues (symptoms) and external cues (health education materials), affect health-related behaviour.

Evaluating strengths and weaknesses of the study

Strengths	Weaknesses
👍 Multiple **methods** (interviews, blood tests) were used to collect data, increasing reliability.	👎 Correlational information was gathered in the **method**. As this only shows a relationship, it is difficult to ascertain cause and effect.
👍 Mothers could and did withdraw their participation, which was **ethical**.	👎 Children were at risk if mothers thought they had low susceptibility to asthma attack, which was not **ethical**.
👍 Shows ways that health behaviours can be predicted and improved.	👎 Only mothers (no fathers) participated, which reduced generalisability to all families.

🌐 Real world Application

Mum Jay and toddler Max were going on holiday when he had an asthma attack. She rushed him to hospital and cancelled the holiday. Max was prescribed both preventer and reliever medication. A family history of asthma meant Jay ensured that Max took the medication.

Becker et al.'s study and the HBM explain high compliance:

- Jay perceived Max's asthma as **serious**, supporting Becker et al.'s findings that perceived seriousness correlates with high compliance.
- The family history suggests Max is **susceptible**, supporting Becker et al.'s findings that susceptibility and compliance correlate.

Now try this

Describe how the cost of Max's asthma attack could influence Jay's compliance. Relate your explanation to Becker et al.'s study and the HBM.

 Consider the cost–benefit aspect of the HBM.

The Carpenter study (2010)

Key study In 'A meta-analysis of the effectiveness of health belief model variables in predicting behavior', Carpenter examines the effectiveness of the **health belief model** (HBM, page 59) in **predicting compliance** with medical advice (medication or behavioural change) in chronic illness.

Key principles of Carpenter (2010)

Aim and procedure

Carpenter thought that the HBM could predict compliance with medical advice.

- The **aim** was to investigate whether people changed their behaviour for treatment or prevention in relation to the HBM aspects.
- In the **procedure** a **meta-analysis** combined several long-term studies.

Analysis included:

- the time between the measurement of the HBM aspects and the health behaviour and whether it was for treatment or prevention
- the percentage who changed behaviour and correlation with the HBM factors.

Findings

1. A small correlation was found between **perceived severity** of a health outcome and adopting the health behaviour; larger if involving **prescription drugs**.
2. Almost no link was found between **perceived susceptibility** and health behaviour.
3. **Perceived benefits** made behavioural change more likely.
4. **Perceived barriers** had the greatest effect on health behaviours, being more significant in prevention than in treatment.
5. As time elapsed between measurement of the HBM variable and the health behaviour, any correlation decreased.

Conclusions

1. The HBM factors vary in their effectiveness at predicting behaviour. Perception of **barriers** and **benefits** were **good predictors**. The other HBM components were poor predictors.

👍 Benefits and barriers should be the focus of interventions as they have most influence on behaviour.

2. The **assumption** that the effectiveness of the HBM in predicting behavioural change decreases with time was supported.

👍 The focus and frequency of health campaigns should take into account that behaviour changes over time.

Evaluating strengths and weaknesses of the study

Strengths	Weaknesses
👍 The **method** used anonymous data.	👎 **Ethics** of original studies were assumed to be appropriate and followed as described.
👍 The meta-analysis gave large amounts of secondary data, allowing for generalisation.	👎 Low validity as quality of studies varied.

🌐 Real world Application

Ravinda is creating a campaign to encourage people with mental health issues to keep to drug regimes, attend counselling, eat well and take exercise. It focuses on the benefits of these actions for health. There is a leaflet, an advice website and an online advert.

When applying Carpenter and the HBM:

- the campaign focuses on the **perceived benefits** of behavioural change
- the campaign repeats the message often. This is helpful because perceived benefits as incentives for change **fade over time**.

Now try this

With reference to the scenario, the HBM and Carpenter's study, suggest another way to support people with depression to make behavioural changes.

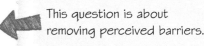 This question is about removing perceived barriers.

Rotter's locus of control

Key theory According to Rotter (1966), the **locus of control** is the degree to which individuals believe they have control over their lives or think that things happen **to** them. Whether a person has an **internal** or **external** locus of control affects their health behaviour. See page 63 for Rotter's study.

Types of locus

People tend to have either an internal or an external locus of control.

- Someone with an **internal locus of control** believes that they can influence events and determine outcomes.
- A person with an **external locus of control** believes events are outside their control and outcomes are decided by external forces.

Locus of control and health decisions

A person's locus of control affects the way they view their health.

- People with an **internal locus** are more likely to make healthy decisions as they believe they can change their health outcomes.
- People with an **external locus** are less likely to make healthy choices as they believe their health is outside their control.

Internal locus of control

Internally controlled individuals:

- believe that their successes are due to their own efforts and abilities
- may have self-belief but are also likely to blame themselves when things go wrong
- may feel confident when faced with the challenge of removing their addiction
- have a strong sense of **self-efficacy** (see page 69) and are less influenced by others' opinions.

External locus of control

Externally controlled individuals:

- believe that outcomes in life are determined by luck, fate and others' actions
- tend to experience anxiety as they don't see themselves as being in control
- are more likely to experience greater impairment from drinking alcohol
- are more influenced by external forces, such as peer pressure.

Locus of control and therapy

- People with an internal locus are more likely to recover from addiction if they feel they have control of their therapy and outcomes.
- People with an external locus of control are more likely to recover if their therapy includes external factors, such as drug rehabilitation.

Real world In the case of stopping smoking, hypnotherapy is more likely to work for internally controlled people as it is something they can do for themselves. Nicotine replacement therapy, an external factor, is more likely to work for externally controlled people.

The role of attribution theory

This is a theory from the **social approach** that explains people's perceptions of the causes of their successes and failures, and what they attribute them to. Causes can be perceived as:

- **internal** (from within the person) or **external** (from outside the person)
- **specific** or **global** (non-specific)
- **stable** (unchanging) or **unstable**
- **controllable** or **uncontrollable**.

 Real world If a person believes they have succeeded in losing weight using willpower, they are more likely to be successful using this method to stop smoking.

 Now try this

Tom gave up smoking but relapsed after his boyfriend left him. He says he started smoking again because his boyfriend treated him badly.

Justify how an external locus of control can explain Tom's smoking relapse.

In a **justify** question, you should give reasons to support the statement used in the question. Remember to link to the source material.

The Rotter study (1966)

Key study In 'Generalised expectancies for internal versus external control of reinforcement', Rotter looked at a range of independent studies to see if their findings supported his **locus of control** theory (see page 62).

Key principles of Rotter (1966)

Aim and procedure

Locus of control can affect whether a person adopts or rejects a health behaviour.

- Rotter's **aim** was to investigate whether internal or external locus of control was more significant in behavioural change.
- The **procedure** involved reviewing several research papers, looking at different behaviours and using the **I–E scale** to measure locus of control.

The I–E scale

Rotter developed the I–E scale.

- Participants are presented with pairs of statements. One represents an internal locus (I) and the other an external locus (E).
- Participants pick the statements they most identify with.
- A score indicates a position on a scale between extremes of internal and external.

Findings

People with an internal locus are:

1 less likely to take risks when gambling, whereas those with an external locus are risk-takers and prone to cognitive biases

2 better at changing other people's attitudes but more resistant to persuasion themselves

3 less likely to smoke and more likely to be successful in quitting if they do

4 less likely to conform to a majority view (using Asch's conformity test, page 11).

Conclusions

Rotter showed that locus of control is a good predictor of a range of behaviours.

Rotter's findings support the **assumption** that locus of control affects health behaviour.

Evaluating strengths and weaknesses of the study

Strengths	Weaknesses
Use of the I–E scale in the **method** gives quantitative data, which are easy to analyse.	It assumed that **ethics** of the original studies were applied.
The study has high applicability to real life as a range of behaviours were considered in the **method**.	The **method** used secondary sources, so there could be issues with reliability.

Real world Application

Luke and Erin are life partners with different outlooks on life. Luke often feels powerless, whereas Erin has strong self-belief.
Erin wants to make some lifestyle changes, including quitting smoking. She has been trying to persuade Luke to join her. He has agreed but he is anxious that he won't be able to change his behaviour.

When applying Rotter:

- Luke has an external locus and Erin has an internal locus
- people with an internal locus, like Erin, are persuasive
- people with an external locus, like Luke, may be more likely to smoke and find it harder to quit.

Now try this

Suggest whether Luke or Erin is more likely to be successful in making this lifestyle change. Refer to the locus of control theory and Rotter's findings in your answer.

Remember to link aspects of the theory, the research findings and information from the scenario.

The Abouserie study (1994)

Key study Stress is a problem for individuals and for society as a whole, due to its effect on health. In **'Sources and levels of stress in relation to locus of control and self-esteem in university students'**, Abouserie investigated causes of stress in relation to **locus of control**. To revise locus of control theory, see page 62.

Key principles of Abouserie (1994)

Aim and procedure

Locus of control affects stress levels.

- The **aim** was to identify sources of stress in university students, to examine gender differences and to consider the roles of locus of control and self-esteem in stress.
- In the **procedure**, a large number of students completed questionnaires about their academic stress, life stress, self-esteem and locus of control.

Findings

1. In students, **academic stress** (exams, essays) was greater than life stress (housing issues).
2. **Females** were more stressed than males.
3. Students with an **external locus** had greater academic stress than those with an internal locus. Differences in life stress were not significant.
4. **Low self-esteem** led to higher stress.

Conclusions

Students are more affected by academic stress than life stress. An external locus of control is associated with higher stress levels and an internal locus with less stress. Counselling can help people take control and move towards an internal locus of control.

Abouserie's findings support his **assumption** that locus of control affects some stresses.

Evaluating strengths and weaknesses of the study

Strengths	Weaknesses
A large sample size in the **method** increased generalisability.	Filling in questionnaires may have caused distress to those already suffering from high levels of stress, which is not **ethical**.
The conclusions show the importance of counselling in coping with academic stress.	In a self-reporting **method**, some people may give socially desirable responses. The students were from one university so results may not apply more widely.

Real world Application

Gabe is revising hard for his psychology exams and reports feelings of extreme stress. He says that no matter how hard he studies, he won't get a good grade as there are always exam questions he hasn't anticipated in his revision.

When applying Abouserie's findings:

- Abouserie found that students reported greater academic stress than life stress. Gabe is feeling academic stress.
- Gabe has an external locus of control as he feels his exam grade is outside his control.
- Abouserie found that people with an external locus, like Gabe, have more academic stress than those with an internal locus.

Now try this

Gabe's tutor thinks that Gabe might benefit from academic counselling.

Suggest how academic counselling might help Gabe. Refer to the locus of control theory and Abouserie's study in your answer.

With professional support, from a counsellor for example, it is possible to change a person's locus of control.

The Krause study (1986)

Key study In **'Stress and coping: reconceptualizing the role of locus of control beliefs'**, Krause looked at depression as a sign of stress, coping mechanisms and **locus of control** in an older population.

Key principles of Krause (1986)

Aim and procedure

Internal locus is usually associated with lower stress. Krause thought that people with **extreme internal locus** may become stressed by attempting to control a situation.

- The **aim** was to study stress and coping mechanisms in relation to locus of control in an **elderly** population.

- The **procedure** involved interviewing retirees aged 65+ from a wide demographic and paying $10 for their participation. Stressful **life events** were measured using a checklist, and locus of control was measured using a version of the **I–E scale** (see page 63).

Findings

1. Older adults with **extreme locus of control** felt greater stress compared to those with moderate locus.

2. Elderly people with **moderate external locus** reported more signs of stress than those with **moderate internal locus**.

3. Those with **extreme internal locus** had better **coping mechanisms** to avoid stress than people with an **extreme external locus**.

Conclusions

Older people with extremes of locus of control exhibit more symptoms of stress than those with moderate locus.

👍 Krause's **assumption** that older people with an extreme internal locus may feel stress is supported by this study.

Evaluating strengths and weaknesses of the study

Strengths	Weaknesses
👍 The **method** used a diverse sample in terms of demographic variables, although it was not racially diverse.	👎 The participants were paid and may have felt unable to withdraw; this is possibly **unethical**.
👍 The conclusions show the importance of taking account of elderly people's locus of control when selecting stress interventions.	👎 Due to self-reporting as a **method**, some may have given socially desirable responses. The sample was limited to one area in the USA and majority white so cannot be generalised.

🌐 Real world Application

Marjory, 80, is downsizing her home. She is quite tearful as the experience is very stressful. She feels that she is no longer capable of making all the necessary arrangements to move house and is relying on her family for help. When Marjory moved in the past, she was always extremely organised and felt in control of events.

When applying Krause:

- Marjory previously felt organised and in control when moving home. This suggests she may have an extreme internal locus of control.

- Krause found that people can feel stressed if they can't control a situation themselves. Marjory is relying on family.

- Krause used depressive symptoms, such as tearfulness, as a measure of stress.

Now try this

Marjory is thinking of visiting her sister while the house move takes place. Discuss Marjory's plan with reference to the locus of control theory and Krause's findings.

Marjory has a plan to remove herself from the source of stress. This is a coping mechanism.

Ajzen's theory of planned behaviour

Key theory The **theory of planned behaviour (TPB)** is a model of behavioural change developed by Ajzen (1985). It supposes that people tend to do what they **plan** to do, and looks at how personal beliefs about the behaviour, what others think and how easy the change is influence the outcome. It can be used to explain addiction and other health behaviours.

Key features

The TPB predicts an individual's intention to participate in a behaviour at a particular time and/or place. The intention to behave in a certain way is driven by **three** aspects:

- the **person's attitude** to the behaviour
- their **subjective norms**
- their **perceived control**.

1 Personal attitude to behaviour

This is the degree to which an individual has **positive** or **negative** views of the behaviour, which could be smoking, gambling, alcohol or drug misuse, or shopping.

Real world Someone who has given up smoking might feel disgust at smoking behaviour in others. A gambler might feel a thrill at the idea of placing a bet.

2 Subjective norms

These are a person's beliefs about what **significant others**, for example partners and family members, think about them and their behaviour.

Real world If there is the expectation that everyone has an alcoholic drink with dinner, it is difficult to abstain. If you and your partner give up drinking together, you will both feel more supported.

3 Perceived behavioural control

This refers to the individual's perception of how easy or difficult it is to carry out behavioural change.

Perceived behavioural control:

- increases when individuals have **resources** (such as treatments and self-belief)
- is influenced by past experience – if you have tried and failed previously, you are more likely to think that you will fail again.

Real world If you believe that you **can** stop smoking, there is a high chance you **will**.

Weakness of TPB

A weakness of TPB is that is doesn't take into account individual factors such as personality, or demographics such as educational level or ethnicity.

Analysis of health decision-making using TPB

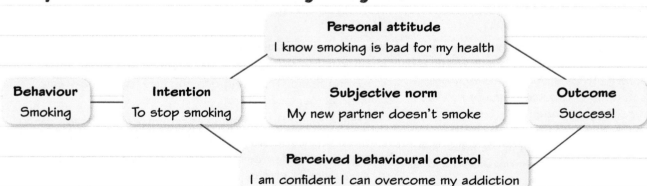

Personal attitude
I know smoking is bad for my health

Behaviour
Smoking

Intention
To stop smoking

Subjective norm
My new partner doesn't smoke

Outcome
Success!

Perceived behavioural control
I am confident I can overcome my addiction

Now try this

Alex likes gambling online as it is easy to do and he often wins, but he feels under pressure from his family to stop participating.

Which aspects of the TPB are influencing Alex?

Identify the parts of the scenario that relate to the three aspects of the model.

The Louis et al. study (2009)

 Key study In **'Stress and the theory of planned behavior: understanding healthy and unhealthy eating intentions'**, Louis et al. tested the **theory of planned behaviour (TBP)** in relation to the effect of stress on eating habits. The theory suggests that intention to act is driven by personal attitude, subjective norms and perceived control (see page 66).

Key principles of Louis et al. (2009)

Aim and method

Louis et al. thought that stress has an effect on the three aspects of the TPB and so would impact on eating intentions.

- The **aim** was to examine life stresses and body-image discrepancy (a psychological stressor) in relation to the TPB.

- In the **method**, student participants, who received a course credit for taking part, completed questionnaires, and height and weight were recorded.

Findings

1. Those with body-image discrepancy intended to eat more unhealthy food.

2. Good **attitudes** to healthy food linked to good intentions.

3. **Perceived control** was associated with low unhealthy-eating and high healthy-eating intentions.

4. Stress altered the impact of the variables, with perceived control being more consistent than subjective norms in terms of unhealthy-eating intentions.

Conclusions

The results of the study provide some support for the TPB, and show that stress has an effect on planned healthy-eating behaviour.

👍 The study supports Louis et al.'s initial **assumption** that stress affects the TPB components.

Evaluating strengths and weaknesses of the study

Strengths	Weaknesses
👍 Using several different **methods** of data collection (questionnaires and objective physical measurements) increases validity.	👎 The **method** used self-reporting data, which are subjective and could produce bias.
👍 Participants were debriefed at the end, which is **ethical**.	👎 The student participants were offered a partial course credit to complete the investigation and may have felt that they couldn't withdraw. This could be **unethical**.

🌐 **Real world** Application

Clive runs the student canteen on a college campus. He has been tasked with improving student eating habits and has decided to focus on promoting the benefits of healthy eating and removing barriers. Students have commented that the prices of fruit and salads are not good value compared to less healthy options, such as chips.

When applying Louis et al.'s study and the TPB:

- TPB identifies personal attitudes, subjective norms and perceived control as drivers of intended behaviour.

- According to Louis et al., a **positive attitude** to healthy eating is linked to healthy-eating intentions. Clive will improve students' attitudes to healthy eating if he promotes the benefits, making it more likely that they will choose healthy options.

Now try this

Discuss the role of barriers in healthy eating. Refer to the scenario, TPB and Louis et al.'s findings.

 Barriers affect a person's perceived control over a planned behaviour.

The Cooke et al. study (2016)

 Key study In their **theory of planned behaviour (TPB)** study, 'How well does the theory of planned behaviour predict alcohol consumption? A systematic review and meta-analysis', Cooke et al. looked at the TPB and another behaviour with negative health consequences, alcohol consumption. The TPB (page 66) can predict behaviours with health benefits, but is usually less accurate in predicting behaviours with negative health consequences.

Key principles of Cooke et al. (2016)

Aim and method

Cooke et al. thought that TPB would be less good at predicting behaviour with negative health consequences.

- The **aim** was to review recent research into TPB and alcohol consumption.

- The **method** was a meta-analysis of lots of studies that measured intention to drink alcohol (within limits, such as to be drunk) or to abstain, against attitudes, subjective norms and perceived control (including self-efficacy).

Findings

1. **Intentions** to drink had a positive correlation with actual alcohol consumption.

2. **Attitudes** had the strongest link with intentions.

3. **Subjective norms** were better at predicting behaviour than **perceived control**.

4. People who have **high confidence** (self-efficacy) in their ability to drink alcohol, intend to and actually do drink more.

Conclusion

The TPB was actually more useful in predicting drinking behaviour than Cooke et al. stated in their starting **assumption**.

Evaluating strengths and weaknesses of the study

Strengths	Weaknesses
The **method** reviewed 40 studies so a lot of data was analysed, increasing validity for generalising results to a wider population.	The idea of 'drinking to get drunk', a category in the **method**, is open to interpretation (it is subjective).
The TPB was shown to be a useful tool for looking at drinking intentions and changing attitudes towards drinking.	Use of other studies assumes that these have been conducted **ethically**.

Real world Application

Matias says he is going to get really drunk with his mates after work. The friends love a drink together and often play drinking games. In the pub, Matias boasts about how many pints of beer he can drink. By the end of the evening, Matias is extremely drunk and one of his friends has to help him home.

When applying the TPB and Cooke et al.:

- Cooke et al. found that the TPB is better than expected at predicting drinking behaviour.

- Matias expressed an intention to drink a lot and did so. The study showed that intentions correlate with consumption.

- The friends enjoy drinking together, which could mean that Matias has a positive personal attitude and positive subjective norms about alcohol. According to Cooke et al., these factors mean he would drink more.

Now try this

1 Which aspect of the scenario suggests that Matias has high self-efficacy in relation to alcohol?

2 According to Cooke et al., what impact does self-efficacy have on drinking alcohol?

 Self-efficacy is an aspect of perceived control.

Bandura's self-efficacy theory

 Key theory Bandura's **self-efficacy theory** (1977) explains an individual's belief in their own ability to change behaviour. Bandura cited mastery experiences, vicarious reinforcement, and the effects of social persuasion and emotional state as important influences.

Key features

Self-efficacy is a person's belief in their ability to influence events and affect life changes. High self-efficacy is helpful in behavioural change, but it can lead to over-confidence.

Self-efficacy is influenced by:

- outcome expectancy
- mastery experiences
- vicarious reinforcement
- social persuasion
- emotional state.

① Outcome expectancy

This is an individual's assessment that a certain behaviour will lead to a particular outcome.

An alcoholic believes that a drink will calm their nerves.

② Mastery experiences

Mastery means experiencing success.

- Having success builds **self-belief**.
- If an individual experiences **failure**, it is important to develop **resilience** by treating the failure as a learning opportunity.

 Real world A gambling addict joins colleagues in a sweepstake but afterwards sees it as a learning opportunity to give up gambling.

③ Vicarious reinforcement

Behaviour is influenced by **observations** of role models.

- If a role model is reinforced for their behaviour, we are likely to imitate them.
- The strength of the influence depends on the similarity between observer and model.

 Real world If an addict observes a peer winning at gambling, they may also want to gamble.

④ Social persuasion

Persuasion by respected others, such as friends and family, can provide a temporary boost in a person's perceived ability to make change. Individuals who receive persuasion are likely to:

- put in more effort and sustain it
- overcome self-doubt.

 Real world If an addict is praised by their counsellor for abstaining from gambling, they will be encouraged to stop completely.

⑤ Emotional state

A person's emotional state is affected by their thinking about the new behaviour.

- Stress, anxiety, worry and fear all negatively affect self-efficacy.
- If stress is reduced and emotional state improves, a change in self-efficacy can be observed.

 Real world If an addict can reduce their anxiety about their gambling behaviour, they are more likely to be able to stop.

Now try this

Sarah's parents smoked when she was a child, so smoking feels normal to her. She knows it is bad for her health, but when she smokes it makes her feel relaxed. She has tried to give up several times in the past but has not succeeded. Her friends think she should give up now, but their pressure is making her feel anxious.

Evaluate Sarah's smoking addiction in terms of self-efficacy theory.

Link aspects of the scenario to the features of the self-efficacy theory.

The Bandura and Adams study (1977)

Key study In their **self-efficacy theory study**, 'Analysis of self-efficacy theory of behavioral **change'**, Bandura and Adams looked at self-efficacy (a person's belief in their ability to make behavioural change) in the treatment of snake phobia by **systematic desensitisation**. In phobias anxiety produces avoidance behaviour. Treatment involves learning relaxation techniques and exposure to a hierarchy of fear, so that avoidance decreases.

Key principles of Bandura and Adams (1977)

Aim and method

Self-efficacy is influenced by outcome expectancy and emotional state (page 69).

- The **aim** was to show that self-efficacy increases and avoidance decreases with reduction in anxiety through treatment.
- In the **method**, participants were treated for snake phobia. Their levels of avoidance, fear and outcome expectancy were scored before and after treatment.

Findings

1. After treatment, self-efficacy was high and positively correlated with more snake interactions and fewer avoidance behaviours.

2. Fear was reduced by the treatment.

Conclusions

Bandura and Adams **concluded** that systematic desensitisation leads to higher levels of self-efficacy and reduced snake phobia.

👍 The findings supported the **assumption** that self-efficacy is important in behavioural change, showing applicability to the treatment of phobias in general.

Evaluating strengths and weaknesses of the study

Strengths	Weaknesses
👍 There was a highly standardised **method**. The same researcher administered the treatment, reducing experimenter bias.	👎 Anxiety was created by the treatment, which could be **unethical**.
👍 Participants were in control of the fear hierarchy, so exposure to anxiety was **ethical**.	👎 In the **method**, the small sample was via a local advert. Therefore participants may have shared characteristics, leading to bias.

🌐 Real world Application

Rafal feels anxious when he thinks about spiders. He sweats and feels sick if he sees one. He is so frightened he thinks he can't change, but a friend persuades him to try a treatment programme. First, Rafal is taught to relax with breathing exercises. Then, over several weeks, he looks at pictures of spiders and lifelike models. Rafal chooses when he is ready to move on to the next spider encounter. Eventually, he thinks he will be able to look at a small living spider.

When applying Bandura and Adams:

- Rafal has low expectancy outcome (he doesn't believe he can change his phobia) and high anxiety, therefore low self-efficacy.
- Bandura and Adams found that anxiety can be replaced by feelings of relaxation, leading to greater self-efficacy.
- Rafal is gradually exposed to a hierarchy of fear, like the one that Bandura and Adams used, and grows in self-efficacy.

Now try this

1 Which aspect of the scenario suggests that treatment improves Rafal's self-efficacy?

2 What is the benefit to Rafal of improved self-efficacy?

 Relate your answers to the self-efficacy theory, and Bandura and Adams' findings.

The Marlatt et al. study (1995)

 Key study In their **self-efficacy theory study, 'Self-efficacy and addictive behavior'**, Marlatt et al. conducted a review into the role of self-efficacy (see page 69) in smoking and drinking.

Types of self-efficacy

Marlatt et al. believed that self-efficacy is critical in behavioural change at all stages of addiction:

- **resistance self-efficacy** – preventing addiction in the first place
- **harm reduction self-efficacy** – ability to moderate behaviour
- **coping self-efficacy** – ability to quit and not relapse
- **recovery self-efficacy** – ability to bounce back after a setback.

Key principles of Marlatt et al. (1995)

Aim and method

- The **aim** was to assess current understanding of self-efficacy and addiction.
- The **method** was a review of previously published articles.

Findings

 Self-efficacy is a factor in all stages of smoking and alcohol addiction.

 Treatments that raise self-efficacy have better outcomes.

 Level of self-efficacy can be used to identify and support those at risk of addiction.

Conclusions

Marlatt et al. **concluded** that preventative interventions should focus on training adolescents to resist social pressure.

👍 The review supported the **assumption** that self-efficacy should be a key feature of the treatment programmes for smokers and alcohol-dependent individuals.

Evaluating strengths and weaknesses of the study

Strengths	Weaknesses
👍 The findings and conclusions have high applicability to prevention and treatment of addiction.	👎 As the study was a review of previous material there may be subjectivity when classifying the intervention strategies.

 Real world Application

Kayden wants to quit smoking but doesn't think he can. Pete doesn't smoke even though all his friends smoke. He is a swimmer and thinks that smoking will affect his performance. Kareem used to smoke heavily but has been successful in his attempts to cut back. Aisha recently quit smoking but was persuaded to have a cigarette after a stressful business meeting. She sees this as a blip and won't let it change her goal to give up.

When applying Marlatt et al. and the self-efficacy theory:

- Kayden has low coping self-efficacy.
- Pete has high resistance self-efficacy.
- Kareem has good harm-resistance self-efficacy.
- Aisha has high recovery self-efficacy.
- According to Marlatt et al., people with high self-efficacy are better at achieving behavioural change.

Now try this

1 Identify the person in the scenario who would most benefit from support to stop smoking.

2 Explain why you selected this person with reference to the theory and study.

For the identify question, just state a name. To answer the explain question, you need to make links between the scenario, theory and study, and justify your argument.

Life events and daily hassles

Life events and daily hassles are **causes of stress**. Research uses self-reporting to look at the effects of these stressors on health. The findings have practical implications for interventions.

 Real world **Life events, daily hassles and uplifts**

- A **life event** is a significant **positive** or **negative** experience that can cause stress. A child's birth is a positive life event. The death of a loved one is a negative life event. Both may cause **psychological stress**.

- **Daily hassles** are minor events that can be a constant source of stress. These can become major events if they are high intensity or high frequency. Examples are missing the bus or not being able to find your house keys.

- **Daily uplifts** are minor positive experiences that counteract daily stress, such as hearing good news.

 Key study **Rahe et al. (1971)**

In **'Prediction of near-future health change from subjects' life changes'**:

- The **aim** was to investigate the link between life events, stress and illness.

- The **method** used a questionnaire, the **Social Readjustment Rating Scale** (SRRS), to ask US Navy servicemen to self-report on the stressful life events experienced during a tour of duty. The number of times they visited the sick bay was also recorded.

- Rahe et al. **found** that sailors who scored low on the questionnaire (few life events) also had low levels of recorded illness.

 Key study **Kanner et al. (1981)**

In **'Comparison of two modes of stress measurement: daily hassles and uplifts versus major life events'**:

- The **aim** was to see if the **Hassles and Uplifts Scale** (HUS) was a good predictor of psychological stress compared to the SRRS.

- The **procedure** used questionnaires to ask men and woman about daily hassles and uplifts, life events and mental health.

- Kanner et al. **found** that daily hassles correlate with psychological symptoms of stress (anxiety and depression) and were a better predictor of stress than life events.

Evaluation of self-reporting

Strengths	Weaknesses
👍 Participants can be asked about feelings and thoughts; not possible with observation.	👎 Gathering information on emotions is only possible if people are willing to disclose.
👍 Qualitative and quantitative data can be gained.	👎 People cope differently with stress, so results can be subjective.
👍 Standardised questions can be used so results are consistent and reliable over time.	👎 It is difficult to infer cause and effect as most methods use correlations.
👍 Both the SRRS and HUS are still used, suggesting self-reporting is a valid method.	👎 People may give socially desirable responses.

 Real world **Application**

- Ranj's mum has died and he is organising the funeral. Ranj is coming down with a cold.

- Frank's car won't start and his computer keeps crashing. Frank feels anxious.

When considering life events, daily hassles and the studies:

- Ranj is experiencing a major life event. These correlate with ill health (Rahe).

- Frank is dealing with daily hassles. These correlate with psychological stress (Kanner).

Now try this

According to Kanner et al., who is likely to experience a greater level of stress – Ranj or Frank?

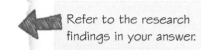 Refer to the research findings in your answer.

Workplace stress

Stress is caused by different aspects of work. Johansson et al. (1978) used a physiological measure and self-reporting to investigate stress in repetitive mechanised work.

Sources of stress in the workplace

 Role conflict

Role conflict is when an individual is expected to perform two incompatible roles.

 Role conflict happens if you have to fire an employee who is a friend.

 Effect of the environment

The working environment includes working hours and physical conditions.

 Long hours and poor conditions cause stress.

 Level of control

Workload is the number of tasks to be completed in a timeframe. The more there are to do in a set time, the bigger the workload. When people **decide** how to do tasks, their order and timescale, they feel less stress. If income level depends on performance, this also contributes to stress.

 In health care, nurses care for patients, and **workload increases** when there are fewer nurses or more patients. In education, if you can **decide** between an essay or a presentation and you are consulted about the deadline, you may be less stressed.

Stress in mechanised work

In mechanisation, machines replace humans. This increases **productivity** but may result in:

- poor conditions and high workload
- jobs with low level of control and repetitive, monotonous tasks but requiring high levels of attention
- stress-related illnesses.

 In modern farming, crops are sewn mechanically. Planting by tractor involves long hours of driving up and down a field with little human contact.

🔍 Key study | Johansson et al. (1978)

In 'Social psychological and neuroendocrine stress reactions in highly mechanised work':

- The **aim** was to measure physiological and psychological stress in employees.
- The **method** measured **adrenaline** in urine (physiological stress indicator) and used a self-rating scale for psychological stress in a high- and a low-risk group of sawmill workers.

- The high-risk group had a poor working environment (with noise, dust and social isolation), greater risk of accident due to inattention and productivity pressure.
- Johansson et al. found that the high-risk group had higher adrenaline and stress levels.

🌐 Real world | Application

Maddy is irritable because life as a dairy farmer and mother is stressful. She is her own boss, but works long hours and often feels she is neglecting her family. Many of Maddy's tasks, such as milking, are repetitive and she spends a lot of time alone.

When applying Johansson et al:

- Sources of stress for Maddy are role conflict, long working hours and time spent alone.
- As her own boss, she has a high level of control, which reduces stress.
- Repetitive work tasks, such as milking, cause physiological and psychological stress.

Now try this

Sion's job is boring. He works alone, inputting data to spreadsheets, has a high workload, frequent deadlines and no control over his tasks.

Suggest how Sion's manager could make his job less stressful.

 Which aspects of workplace stress are relevant to Sion?

Personality and stress

Personality type is an important factor in how individuals respond to stress.

Personality types

Some personality types are:

- hardy personality
- Type A
- Type B.

Individual reactions to stress

People react differently to stress due to their:

- genes
- tolerance to physiological stress
- thinking patterns about the stressor.

Hardy personality

Hardiness provides resilience against stress. A hardy personality can be explained in terms of **commitment**, **control** and **challenge**.

 A learner with a hardy personality:

- **has commitment** – tackles problems head on, with purpose. This learner participates in class, meets deadlines, revises for tests and gains good grades.
- **takes control** – takes charge of situations. This learner is responsible for leading a team project.
- **meets a challenge** – sees situations as opportunities rather than threats. This learner would not be stressed by a teacher's departure, but sees potential in having a new teacher.

Comparing Type A and B personalities

Type A personality	Type B personality
Ambitious, impatient, competitive, hostile	Relaxed, patient and easy-going
Prone to stress from impatience	Less prone to stress as more relaxed
Long-term stress causes susceptibility to high blood pressure and coronary heart disease	Fewer stress-related health problems than Type A people
Suited to fast-paced and competitive employment roles, such as sales jobs	Suited to roles requiring patience, such as caring
Tends to multi-task	Tends to focus on one task at a time
Real world Type A individuals may strive to be the best trader on the floor, or overact if they spill a drink.	Real world Type B individuals are likely to wait until the deadline before chasing people up.

 Application

Students are revising for final exams.

- Kai is finding it hard to settle to revision, and just wants his exams to be over.
- Caitlin has devised a revision timetable, is working hard and has been to see her teacher about the areas she finds difficult.
- Jade hasn't started revising yet and thinks there's still plenty of time.

When considering personality types and individual responses to stress:

- Kai's impatience suggests he has a Type A personality. He is probably very stressed.
- Caitlin is demonstrating control, commitment and challenge, so has a hardy personality. She will be resilient to stress.
- Jade's relaxed attitude is typical of a Type B personality, and she probably isn't stressed.

Now try this

The football coach notices team members' different reactions when the cup final is mentioned.

Describe how Type A, Type B and hardy personalities in the team may react to the stress of playing in the approaching cup final.

 Make sure you cover all three identified personality types.

General adaptation syndrome

The **general adaptation syndrome (GAS)** is a model for the body's **physiological** response to stress. Short-term stress can improve performance, whereas long-term stress can cause health problems.

Body systems and stress

The response to stress involves two body systems:

- the **autonomic nervous system** (ANS), which directs body functions that are not under conscious control
- the **endocrine system**, which controls body functions by releasing hormones.

Function of the ANS

The ANS has two parts:

- **sympathetic nervous system** (SNS), which stimulates body functions and is associated with the **fight-or-flight response**.
- **parasympathetic nervous system** (PNS), which slows down body functions, conserves energy and is associated with rest and sleep.

Fight-or-flight response

Our body systems have evolved to work together to enable us to cope with danger.

- In modern life we rarely face the types of dangers our early ancestors faced that this response evolved to counter. However, our bodies still respond to stressors by preparing for **aggression** (fight) or to **escape** danger (flight).
- When faced with a stressor, the **SNS** communicates with the **endocrine system**, which responds by releasing **hormones**.
- In turn, these hormones act on other parts of the SNS to speed up body systems to bring about the fight-or-flight response (see page 76).

Three stages of the GAS

The GAS describes three stages of stress response.

 1 **Alarm reaction**
In the first stage of the GAS, the mechanism to deal with the stressor is activated and the fight-or-flight response begins. For example, heart rate increases and there is an energy boost.

 2 **Resistance**
In the second stage, the body slowly returns to its previous physiological state. If stress is **prolonged**, most fight-or-flight responses decrease, but **cortisol** production increases (see page 77). This allows the body to continue to resist the stressor.

 3 **Exhaustion**
If stress continues long term, the body cannot return to a typical state. In this third stage, resources are used up, leading to exhaustion. The body can't fight the stress and a weakened immune system may lead to illness (see page 83).

 Real world **Application**

On the first day of a new job, Steve can feel his heart racing and he has lots of energy.

As he gradually settles into the job, he feels more normal again.

When applying the stages of the GAS:

- Starting a new job is stressful and Steve is feeling the alarm reaction stage of the GAS.
- As Steve settles into his job, his body normalises (resistance phase).

Now try this

What are the consequences for Steve if his job is stressful in the long term? Refer to the GAS in your answer.

 This question is about the second and third stages of the GAS.

Sympathomedullary pathway

The **sympathomedullary (SAM)** pathway plays a role in the body's response to acute stress. It controls the alarm reaction phase of the GAS (see page 75).

Acute stress

Acute stress is a short-term experience. It usually results from an event or situation that is new or unexpected. Acute stress brings about the **fight-or-flight response** (see page 75).

 Real world Your first day at college is a new experience. Someone stealing your mobile phone is unexpected. Both cause short-term stress.

Role of SAM pathway in acute stress

When a stressor is present:

1 the brain's hypothalamus activates the sympathetic nervous system (SNS)

2 the SNS stimulates the **adrenal glands**, releasing **cortisol**, **adrenaline** (epinephrine) and **noradrenaline** (norepinephrine)

3 adrenaline and noradrenaline stimulate the SNS to activate organs for fight or flight. Cortisol increases blood sugar.

Adrenal glands

- The adrenal glands are located on the top of each kidney.
- Each gland is split into an **adrenal cortex** (outer part) and an **adrenal medulla** (inner part).
- Cortisol is made in the adrenal cortex.
- Adrenaline and noradrenaline are made in the adrenal medulla.

Stress hormones

These hormones are involved in fight or flight:

- **Adrenaline** increases heart rate and redistributes blood to the brain for fast reactions and to skeletal muscles for movement.
- **Noradrenaline** narrows blood vessels to raise blood pressure and improve circulatory efficiency.
- **Cortisol** is involved in the regulation of blood sugar for energy production.

Short-term effects of stress hormones

Physical signs of the fight-or-flight response for acute stress include:

- rapid heart and breathing rate
- increased blood pressure
- pale or flushed skin and sweating
- dry mouth
- muscle tension and trembling
- dilated (enlarged) pupils and tunnel vision.

🌐 **Real world Application**

Imani is taking part in a sprint race.

She is really nervous on the starting blocks, but pulls away fast as the starting gun fires.

She begins well, keeps up a great pace, runs her best time and finishes first.

In response to nerves about the race, Imani's performance will improve as her body is prepared for flight.

- Cortisol will increase her blood sugar, providing extra energy for her muscles.
- Adrenaline directs the blood to her brain for a quick reaction to the starting gun and to her muscles for a powerful run.
- Her heart and breathing rate also increase, meaning that she can run faster.

Now try this

Using an example, define the term 'acute stress'.

 You could make a link to an example from your daily life, for example from college or a part-time job.

Hypothalamic-pituitary-adrenal system

The body responds to chronic stress via the **hypothalamic-pituitary-adrenal system (HPA)**. Chronic stress is experienced in stages 2 and 3 of the general adaptation syndrome (see page 75). Prolonged stress causes different physiological responses compared to acute stress.

Chronic stress

This occurs in response to a challenging long-term situation or through repeated exposure to a stressor. Chronic stress is exhausting for mind and body.

Real world If you are studying a difficult subject, struggling in lessons and performing poorly in tests, you may feel chronic stress.

Cortisol

Cortisol **level** naturally increases and decreases throughout the day. In chronic stress, the cortisol level within the blood increases and remains high.

Role of the HPA in chronic stress

1 Chronic stress is detected in the **hypothalamus** of the brain.

2 The hypothalamus activates the **pituitary gland** in the brain to produce **ACHT** (adrenocorticotropic hormone).

3 This in turn stimulates the **adrenal cortex** of the **adrenal glands** to produce **cortisol**.

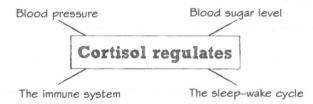

Blood pressure   Blood sugar level

Cortisol regulates

The immune system   The sleep–wake cycle

Long-term effects of cortisol exposure

A high level of cortisol is associated with these **physical** problems:

- high blood pressure and heart disease
- muscle weakness and headaches
- poor immune function and healing
- digestive problems and weight gain.

Psychological effects include:

- deterioration of cognitive skills and memory
- anxiety and depression
- sleep disruption.

Individual reactions to stress

Individuals react differently to stress:

- **Genetics** can influence how people react. Overactive or underactive stress responses may result from slight variations in genes.
- **Life experiences** influence the stress response. Events in early life, such as abuse, can make individuals more vulnerable to stress.
- Some **occupations** are more stressful than others. Jobs in the armed forces and emergency services are stressful.

Coping with stress

Acknowledging the causes of stress and understanding the body's physiological reactions are helpful in stress management. Management techniques include:

- eating a healthy diet
- meditation, hobbies and exercise.

Exercise can be a successful stress management technique.

Now try this

Daisy is an officer in the army. She has chronic stress and a high level of cortisol in her blood.

Suggest some of the effects on Daisy of having chronic stress.

Remember that there are both psychological and physiological effects of chronic stress.

Role of adrenaline

The hormone **adrenaline** is produced in the adrenal glands of the kidneys. It controls the body's fight-or-flight response to stress and is active in the SAM pathway (see page 76).

Adrenaline and stress

Adrenaline is released from the adrenal medulla of the adrenal glands. It plays a part in:

- increasing heart rate
- raising blood pressure
- expanding the lungs
- dilating the pupils of the eyes
- redistributing blood to the muscles.

Physiological effects of adrenaline

People feel the effects of adrenaline when faced with a stressor.

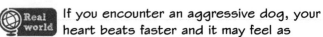 If you encounter an aggressive dog, your heart beats faster and it may feel as though it is about to burst through your chest wall. Your blood pressure also increases. Your breathing becomes fast and shallow. You may feel hot and sweaty as your body temperature increases.

Adrenaline as a drug treatment

Adrenaline is used to treat people with extreme allergic reactions (anaphylactic shock).

- It relaxes the muscles around the airways within the lungs, helping the airways to open for more effective breathing.
- It also prevents release of more allergic chemicals by the body in response to the allergen.

Adrenaline, delivered by an auto-injecting device called an Epipen, is used to treat anaphylactic shock.

Use of beta blockers

Beta blockers are medicines that **block the effects of adrenaline.** They:

- reduce blood pressure by relaxing blood vessels
- prevent adrenaline stimulating the heart receptors that make the heart pump faster
- are prescribed for anxiety, high blood pressure and angina (a heart disorder) for example.

Noradrenaline

Noradrenaline is released as a hormone from the adrenal medulla of the adrenal glands, but also within the cardiovascular nerves of the sympathetic nervous system, where it functions as a neurotransmitter. It constricts (narrows) blood vessels to increase blood pressure and also helps to increase blood sugar level.

Now try this

Oliver is so nervous about his exams that it is affecting his health. Frequently, he feels his heart pounding and gets hot and sweaty.

Suggest **one** reason why Oliver may be prescribed beta blockers to help him deal with the stress of his exams.

 You should give a reason for the use of beta blockers in this scenario. Remember that beta blockers reduce the effects of adrenaline.

Physiological gender differences

There are gender differences in physiological responses to stress. Individuals of different gender may display **different** physiological responses to the **same** stressors or they may have the **same** physiological response but **behave** differently. It would be limiting to view stress purely as a physiological response.

Adrenaline – increases blood flow to muscles in the fight-or-flight response (see page 76)

Cortisol – regulates immune response and metabolic rate (see page 77)

The four key hormones released in response to stress

Testosterone – reduces effect of oxytocin; males usually have higher levels

Oxytocin – promotes bonding and sociability; females usually have higher levels

Responses to stress

Individuals of different gender tend to have slightly different physiological stress responses and different behavioural responses, some of which may be learned.

- Those with more **testosterone** (often males) tend to act on the fight-or-flight response, and may instinctively demonstrate aggression towards the threat or move away from it.
- Those with more **oxytocin** (often females) tend to show a 'tend-and-befriend' response, and may talk their way out of danger rather than fighting or running.

Stress reactivity

Some research into gender differences in response to stressful situations has suggested the following general outcomes.

- Those with a more emotional, irritable and fearful response to stress tended to be female.
- Those more likely to be stressed about relationships, finance and work tended to be male. Those more likely to be stressed about family and health issues tended to be female.
- Those with rational and detached coping styles tended to be male, while those with emotional and avoidance coping styles tended to be female.
- Those more open to reporting the effects of stress tended to be female.

Genetic differences

The different genetic make-up reflected in individuals of different gender helps to explain why they respond differently to stress. Production of the hormones testosterone and oxytocin is controlled by genes. The differences in behaviour may be **evolutionary adaptations** as traditionally:

- males evolved as hunters and protectors, so the fight-or-flight response would have been advantageous to them.
- nursing females could not escape danger in the same way as males, so evolved calming behaviours.

Limitations

There are limitations in viewing stress as a purely physiological condition mediated by the GAS, SAM and HPA systems.

- Although stress is influenced by hormones, these are present in different amounts in individuals of different gender.
- People of the same gender may respond differently to the same stressors.
- Historically, there may be evolutionary reasons for different behaviours in different genders.
- Responses to stress and associated behaviour may reflect physiological gender differences and may also be learned or contributed to by other factors such as cognition (page 80) or personality (page 82).

Now try this

The company Diane and Matt work for is making redundancies. They are both very stressed. Diane is not sleeping well and is eating lots of chocolate. Matt is playing football every night. He has been sent off for dangerous tackles and arguing with the referee.

Explain Diane and Matt's responses to stress and why it may be a weakness to view it as a purely physiological response.

Freeze response

There are more than two physiological responses to stress. Alongside the fight-or-flight response (see page 75) is the **freeze** response and the **role of cognitions** in this response.

Multiple responses

The physiological changes that lead to the fight-or-flight response can lead to a third response, the **freeze response**.

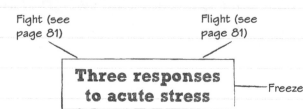

Fight (see page 81)   Flight (see page 81)

Three responses to acute stress — Freeze

The freeze response to stress

The freeze response to stress can happen when an individual is faced with a stressor or danger. Instead of running away or staying to fight the stressor, the person experiences a temporary paralysis.

If you are involved in a car accident, you may be temporally 'frozen to the spot' before being able to get out of the vehicle to see if everyone else is all right.

Role of cognitions in the freeze response

Cognitive functions are thinking, perceiving, understanding and remembering.

Extreme acute stress causes over-arousal, which affects these processes. It limits cognitive capacity and so creates a moment in which events can't be interpreted and understood, and there is severe indecision about the correct course of action. This is 'cognitive paralysis' or the freeze response.

Limitations

The three very different responses of fight, flight and freeze suggest there is more to stress than a purely physiological response that is the same in everyone.

- Cognitions are involved in responses to stress, so stress can't be simply physiological.
- Viewing stress as a purely physiological condition mediated by the GAS, SAM and HPA systems, which are broadly similar in all people, does not take into consideration different final reactions.

Now try this

Dave, Sajii and Stu are involved in a collision with another car. Dave, the driver, runs from the scene. Sajii gets into an altercation with the driver of the other car and Stu stays still in the back seat.

Explain the reactions of Dave, Sajii and Stu and why it may be a weakness to view them as a purely physiological response.

Consider how these individuals are demonstrating the three different reactions to acute stress.

Fight-or-flight response

The fight-or-flight response is **maladaptive** in modern society, which demonstrates a limitation of viewing stress as a purely physiological response. It is a response to danger from the environment of evolutionary adaptation which is no longer suitable for the experiences of modern life.

Fight-or-flight response

The fight-or-flight response results from physiological changes that occur when a threat is present (see page 75).

- The response is triggered in the sympathetic nervous system when adrenaline, noradrenaline and cortisol are released from the adrenal glands (see page 76).
- The fight-or-flight response evolved to deal with stressful threats in prehistoric times.

The fight-or-flight response is useful when faced with immediate physical danger, such as when a prey needs to outrun or defend itself against a predator.

A maladaptive response

The fight-or-flight response is maladaptive in modern society.

- The stressors in society today are different from prehistoric stressors. Fight or flight is an unsuitable response to the stresses that most humans face in their everyday lives.
- As stress activates the fight-or-flight response more regularly, it puts strain on vital organs and body systems.

Effects on health

The fight-or-flight response is no longer beneficial as it is unhealthy in situations of more continual stress. Effects on health of the maladaptive fight-or-flight response include:

- **physiological** – stress-induced aggravation of painful conditions such as backache, fibromyalgia and osteoporosis
- **psychological** – heightened anxiety and depressive feelings.

Maladaptive response behaviours

A maladaptive response is a behaviour that inhibits an individual's ability to adjust to the current situation and stressors.

 Real world Going on a shopping spree may allow you to forget about the stress of your college work, but the effects are only temporary. When you look at the bags full of shopping and realise that you still have deadlines, the stress returns, perhaps even worse than before.

Limitations

The poor match of the fight-or-flight behaviours to modern-day stress show that there are evolutionary (genetic) reasons for the behaviour, and therefore limitations in viewing stress as only a physiological response.

Now try this

Freda is relocating for work. She is trying to sell her home, buy a new house and start a new job. She is so stressed that she is experiencing anxiety attacks.

Explain Freda's response to her stressful circumstances and the limitation of viewing stress as purely a fight-or-flight physiological response.

Consider how Freda is experiencing a maladaptive response to stress, and the effect of the fight-or-flight physiological changes in her body in a situation where there is no quick solution to the stress.

Role of personality

There is a limitation in viewing stress as a purely physiological response, given the role of personality in stress responses. Individuals show variation in hormone types and levels, influencing personality.

Personality types

Personality is shaped by genetics, social influences and personal experiences. There are several personality types (see page 74).

- Type As are driven and competitive individuals.
- Type Bs are generally laid back.
- Hardy personalities are committed to their tasks.

Personality and stress

Personality type has implications for an individual's response to stress.

- Type A personalities do not cope well with stress. They may have tense facial muscles and aggressive speech patterns.
- Type B and hardy personalities cope better with stress, experiencing fewer hassles than Type A personalities.

Variation in hormones

There are differences in the types and levels of hormones released by individuals in stress.

- Some individuals are more vulnerable to type 2 diabetes. Their livers may release more glucose as a response to cortisol and adrenaline.
- In males, excessive amounts of cortisol can affect testosterone production and sperm production, leading to impotence.
- In females, stress can affect the menstrual cycle and increase the symptoms of premenstrual syndrome (PMS) due to testosterone and cortisol.

Variation in stress response

Other factors can play a role in explaining variations in stress response:

- Individuals who use an emotion-focused strategy for dealing with stress may be ineffective as they don't address the cause of the stress. Some women tend to use more emotion-focused strategies for managing stress than males.
- Type B personalities with positive expectations may use a more successful problem-focused strategy for managing stress.

Limitations

The effect of personality types on stress can be seen as offering a complementary explanation to a purely physiological explanation of stress.

A person's personality, as well as their physiology, influences how they react to stress.

Now try this

Li Wei has a Type A personality and dislikes delivering presentations. The college principal has asked him and his friend Claire, Type B, to give a presentation to a local school to promote the college and the courses it offers.

Explain how Li Wei's response in this stressful situation would be different from Claire's response.

You could include behaviours that might be observed by the school students.

Stress and ill health

Stress causes ill health due to suppression of the immune system. Kiecolt-Glaser et al. (1984) demonstrated that stress affects the body's ability to fight infection.

Immune system

The immune system is made up of the organs and cells that protect against disease-causing agents (**pathogens**), such as bacteria and viruses.

- **White blood cells** (leukocytes) travel around the body through the blood vessels.
- When white cells recognise a pathogen by its unique surface proteins (**antigens**), they destroy it.
- Some white cells produce binding proteins (**antibodies**) that attach to antigens, signalling to other white cells to kill the pathogen.
- Some white cells engulf (enclose) pathogens to destroy them.

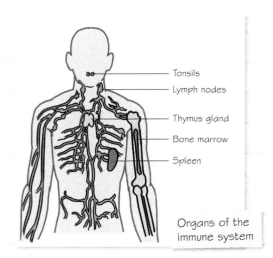

Tonsils
Lymph nodes
Thymus gland
Bone marrow
Spleen

Organs of the immune system

Stress and cortisol

Stress causes the release of cortisol (see page 77). Cortisol affects the immune system.

- Short-term exposure to cortisol **boosts** the immune system, reducing inflammation.
- Long-term exposure to cortisol reduces the number of white cells. The lower the number of these cells, the greater the risk of catching an illness such as a cold.

 If you are worried about an exam, you may catch a cold.

Long-term immunosuppression

Long-term exposure to cortisol through chronic stress can seriously interfere with the immune system, causing **immunosuppression**.

 Immunosuppressed individuals are at greater risk of cancer, heart disease and diabetes, as well as many minor infections.

The Kiecolt-Glaser et al. (1984) study

In 'Psychosocial modifiers of immunocompetence in medical students':

- The **aim** was to see whether the stress caused by important exams affected students' immune systems.
- The **method** measured white cell counts and used self-report questionnaires to assess stress, loneliness and life events.

- **Findings** included lower white cell counts during exams compared to one month before, and lower white cell counts in those reporting stress, loneliness and more life events.
- The **conclusion** was that the stress of exams, loneliness and life events all reduced the effectiveness of the immune system.

Now try this

Jenny, who is about to sit her psychology exam, feels she is coming down with a cold. She doesn't understand how she can be getting a cold now as she had been feeling healthy until the start of the exam period.

Explain why Jenny feels ill around exam time, using your understanding of the Kiecolt-Glaser et al. (1984) study.

 Refer to the effects of stress on the immune system.

Stress and the cardiac system

Long-term stress increases the chances of developing cardiovascular diseases such as high blood pressure, hardened arteries and coronary heart disease (CHD).

Function of a healthy cardiac system

A healthy cardiac system transports nutrients, hormones and oxygen throughout the body, and removes waste products. It also protects the body by:

- transporting white blood cells, which defend against pathogens and toxins
- regulating body temperature
- maintaining pH level
- ensuring the correct balance of water in cells and tissues.

Short-term effects of adrenaline

Acute stress causes the release of adrenaline (see page 76). In the short term, adrenaline makes the heart work harder as it:

- increases heart rate (beats per minute)
- causes stronger heart muscle contractions
- causes some blood vessels (such as skeletal vessels) to dilate and some (such as those of the digestive system) to constrict, overall elevating blood pressure.

Long-term effects of adrenaline

Long-term exposure to adrenaline as a result of stress leads to an increased risk of:

- hypertension (high blood pressure)
- CHD and stroke
- aneurysm (a bulge or swelling within a blood vessel, such as the aorta, due to the extra strain on the vessel wall).

Long-term effects of cortisol

People with elevated cortisol due to chronic stress (see page 77) are five times more likely to die from heart attacks, strokes or other cardiovascular conditions.

- Cortisol and adrenaline combined have a damaging effect on the cardiac system.
- When arteries become constricted and there is an increase in blood pressure, plaque can build up, leading to heart attack or stroke.

Unhealthy lifestyle choices

Stress can influence behaviour and lead to unhealthy lifestyle choices, which cause ill health. Smoking, eating junk food and lack of physical activity can all increase blood pressure and damage arteries. The reasons people give for making unhealthy lifestyle choices include:

- lack of time to cook healthy meals from scratch or to exercise
- needing the relaxation that comes with a cigarette or alcoholic drink after the stress of a busy day.

Effects of lifestyle choices

Lifestyle choices are influenced by stress and can affect health.

- Exercise releases endorphins which reduce blood pressure, while lack of exercise increases blood pressure and damages the cardiac system.
- A glass of wine may be relaxing but, if a person **needs** alcohol to relax, an unhealthy relationship may be formed leading to reliance on alcohol and addiction.
- Comfort-eating, an emotional response to stress, can lead to blood-sugar imbalance and an increased risk of diabetes.

Now try this

Priya has worked in a highly stressful job for many years. She works long hours, has little time for exercise and often eats takeaway meals.

Suggest **one** effect that long-term stress and lifestyle choices could have on Priya's cardiac function.

You only need to suggest one effect, but you should link it to all the factors in the scenario.

Biological approach to smoking

The key principles of physiological addiction include **initiation**, **maintenance** and **relapse**. The **biological** approach to **addiction to smoking** focuses on innate factors that influence behaviour, such as physiology and genetics.

Physiological addiction to nicotine

Nicotine is the main addictive chemical in cigarettes, although research suggests that other chemicals in tobacco smoke also contribute. Nicotine stimulates the brain so that adrenaline is released from the adrenal glands, which raises pulse rate and blood pressure. Side effects of nicotine (headache and dizziness) decrease the longer a person smokes.

Predisposition to smoking addiction

Some researchers suggest that the DRD2 gene could be partly responsible for addiction in some individuals who try smoking, repeat the behaviour and become regular smokers.

However, other researchers suggest there is not one specific gene but several genes that cause an individual to be more susceptible to nicotine addiction, including genetic vulnerability to addictive behaviours in response to stressors.

 Key study **Vink et al. (2005)**

In '**Heritability of smoking initiation and nicotine dependence**':

- The **aim** was to investigate the genetic and environmental factors in smoking initiation and nicotine dependence.
- The **method** used a twin study.
- The **findings** indicated that nicotine dependence is largely influenced by genetic factors and partly by other factors.

1 Initiation

People **start** smoking cigarettes because nicotine:

- boosts mood and reduces irritability by stimulating **dopamine** release and the brain's reward system
- has both a stimulating and a calming effect; it provides an initial 'kick' and then a sedative effect.

2 Maintenance

People **continue** to smoke:

- to maintain the effect of dopamine
- due to tolerance (more of the drug needed for the same effect)
- because they have negative sensations without cigarettes, which can be regulated by smoking.

3 Relapse

People may **relapse** to avoid the negative consequences of not smoking. Symptoms of nicotine withdrawal can be:

- **physical**, such as shaking, headaches, vomiting, sweating
- **psychological**, such as cravings, anxiety, depression, difficulty in concentrating.

Evaluating the biological approach to explaining behaviour

Strengths	Weaknesses
👍 A biological approach to nicotine addiction focuses on **changes in brain neurochemistry**. This is an objective and scientific explanation of addiction.	👎 The biological approach ignores the role of behavioural factors in addiction and could, therefore, be seen as reductionist.
👍 Another biological explanation of smoking addiction is **genetics**. This is also an objective and testable explanation of addiction.	👎 In Vink et al.'s study, genetics was not the only factor that caused addiction. This suggests involvement of other factors, such as environmental or social situations as well.

 Now try this

Olivia, a smoker, and Helena, a non-smoker, are identical twins.

Discuss whether Helena might start to smoke, due to her genes. Refer to the findings of Vink et al. in your answer.

 Remember that identical twins have the same genes.

85

Learning approach to smoking

The **learning** approach to **addiction to smoking** focuses on **behaviour** as a product of learning that involves observing and imitating people, being rewarded through positive reinforcement, and conditioned response behaviour, for example. It offers perspectives on smoking and the **three** key principles of physiological addiction.

① Initiation

The learning approach suggests that starting to smoke can be explained by:

- **social learning theory:** where individuals may observe adults and role models smoking, make a positive association and imitate them. If a role model experiences positive reinforcement when smoking (e.g. popularity), an individual may seek the same result if they smoke (**vicarious reinforcement**).

- **operant conditioning:** where peers might encourage smoking so the person experiences positive reinforcement by the reward of acceptance along with stress relief, for example.

- **classical conditioning:** where an association is made between smoking and increased mood, creating conditioned response behaviour.

③ Relapse

Relapses in smoking behaviour may be explained by the learning approach. For example:

- the continuation of **operant conditioning** processes in the context of withdrawal symptoms.

- the continuation of **classical conditioning** ideas where smoking can become associated with a **cue** (an activity or environment) that triggers conditioned response behaviour.

 Drinking coffee can trigger a craving to smoke, if a link has been established.

② Maintenance

Concepts from the learning approach explain why people continue to smoke. For example:

- the ideas of **operant conditioning** and the continuing reward element of smoking, alongside **negative reinforcement** where, by continuing to smoke, the smoker stops unpleasant withdrawal symptoms such as anxiety, low mood and irritability.

- the ideas of **classical conditioning** and the continued association of nicotine with **sensory information** from other pleasurable activities.

 Drinking alcohol and socialising with certain groups of friends may become associated with cigarette smoking.

Self-efficacy and smoking cessation

Self-efficacy has an important role in the cessation of smoking and avoidance of relapse. Self-efficacy is the individual's belief in their own ability to meet a challenge.

 People with low self-efficacy may doubt their ability to succeed in giving up, and may relapse into smoking behaviours.

Evaluating the learning approach to explaining behaviour

Strengths	Weaknesses
👍 Treatments based on the learning approach, such as aversion therapies where negative associations are formed with smoking, have been shown to be successful in treating addiction.	👎 The learning approach highlights the role of the environment but ignores the biological aspects of addiction, such as the dopamine reward system in the brain.
👍 Secondary reinforcers (items that are associated with cigarettes, such as cigarette boxes and lighters) can trigger cravings and relapse in addicts, highlighting the role of the learning approach concepts in addiction.	👎 Most of the rewards of smoking described by the learning approach, such as behavioural reinforcement from peers, are short-term and so do not offer a complete explanation of long-term behaviour.

Now try this

Dannie's parents and siblings all smoke.

Explain why Dannie may start smoking, using your knowledge of the learning approach.

 Your answer must contain reasons for or justification of the behaviour.

Cognitive approach to alcohol

The **cognitive** approach to **alcohol addiction** suggests that faulty cognitions (ways of processing information) are responsible for the initiation, maintenance and relapse of behaviour.

Self-medication model

Individuals use alcohol to mitigate physical and psychological problems, such as pain or anxiety.

- Drinking alcohol suppresses the brain activity associated with these and other problems.
- In the long term, alcohol is decreasingly effective at alleviating symptoms, so people tend to drink more to self-medicate.

1 Initiation

People often use alcohol to self-medicate, as mitigation for an issue that has not been treated, or for a specific effect.

- Individuals who experienced trauma may self-medicate to avoid the ongoing feelings associated with the trauma.
- Anxious people may use alcohol to produce feelings of relaxation. Aggressive people may seek opiates to stabilise their mood.
- People drink to manage chronic pain.

2 Maintenance

People need increasing amounts of alcohol in order to obtain the self-medication effects they seek. They assume it is helping to manage problems or associate it with stress relief, so maintain their addiction. As alcohol is a depressant, it can make the symptoms of anxiety worse.

If an alcoholic believes the drug is working to help their anxiety, but it is actually increasing the symptoms, their drinking will escalate.

3 Relapse

Individuals need to have control over their actions to give up alcohol and avoid relapse.

- **Cognitive dissonance** is a conflict in balancing beliefs. If someone **thinks** they want to stop drinking but **believes** they can't, they may relapse.
- If someone has been using alcohol to self-medicate, they need an alternative way to address their underlying problems.
- Whether someone is successful in remaining alcohol-free depends on having **self-efficacy** – belief in their own coping strategies for side effects, for example (see page 69).

- Having an **internal locus of control** (see page 62) with a strong sense of being able to control events, helps avoid relapse.
- It is **counterproductive** to recovery if the individual tries to numb the emotion of an event such as a new job or meeting new people by drinking alcohol, or if they think their problems are solved so return to alcohol.
- **Stress levels** can have implications for relapse. An increase in anxiety due to withdrawal increases the risk of relapse.

Evaluating the cognitive approach to explaining behaviour

Strengths	Weaknesses
👍 Faulty thinking and anxiety are cognitive states that can explain alcohol addiction. The self-medication model suggests that, if problems are relieved, addiction improves.	👎 The cognitive approach to alcohol addiction does not include neurochemical responses to the drug (physiology).
👍 Alcoholics may rationalise their behaviour. Therefore, cognitive behavioural therapies can be used to treat addiction.	👎 It can be difficult to establish cause and effect between faulty thinking and alcohol addiction (e.g. unclear which comes first).

Now try this

Kara is a negotiator in an advertising agency. She negotiates contracts with clients over dinner and is drinking more alcohol to get through these meals.

Describe **one** reason for Kara's dependency on alcohol, using your knowledge of the cognitive approach.

 Your response to a **describe** question needs to be developed. Make sure that you link to the scenario throughout your answer.

Learning approach to alcohol

The **learning** approach explains substance misuse in terms of learning from environmental factors such as role models, punishments and rewards.

Operant conditioning in alcohol addiction

In operant conditioning, rewards and punishments shape actions.

- Where actions produce a direct reward (positive reinforcement), behaviour is repeated.
- Where actions lead to unpleasant consequences, behaviour is likely to stop.

Role models in alcohol addiction

Role models can shape behaviour in the early stages of addiction.

 Real world If colleagues you admire go to the pub every night after work, you may want to join them to socialise and appear a team player.

① Initiation

Alcohol addiction can involve positive and negative reinforcement, and the influence of role models.

- Individuals use alcohol to **relax**. It activates the **dopamine** reward pathway within the brain, which makes the individual feel good.
- Addiction develops if the individual keeps drinking in order to feel this way again (**positive reinforcement**).

- **Negative reinforcement** strengthens behaviour that reduces unpleasant outcomes. Drinking alcohol can remove feelings of **stress**.
- If a celebrity **role model** advertises an alcoholic product, an individual may imitate them in the hope of gaining the same rewards, such as popularity.

② Maintenance

Drinking stops negative feelings, at least temporarily. **Negative reinforcement** of alcohol use means drinking behaviour is repeated. Maintenance of alcohol use avoids:

- physiological **withdrawal symptoms** (headaches, hallucinations and sweating)
- psychological withdrawal symptoms (irritability and insomnia).

③ Relapse

Relapsing into alcohol use causes **withdrawal symptoms** to cease, so resumption of drinking is also **negatively reinforced**.

Individuals may relapse for different reasons:

- being in a restaurant or bar where others are consuming alcohol
- being unable to cope with stress
- drinking to numb feelings of trauma.

Evaluating the learning approach to explaining behaviour

Strengths	Weaknesses
👍 Aversion therapy can associate alcohol with a negative experience, such as vomiting. However, if the new association is not maintained, relapse can occur.	👎 The learning approach ignores the role of biology in behaviour. For example, prolonged use of alcohol can cause physiological illness.
👍 Learning theories can be scientifically tested, such as Rotter (1966, page 63) and Bandura and Adams (1977, page 70).	👎 Some therapies from the learning approach are seen as unethical and can be dangerous. In aversion therapy, participants can become distressed by vomiting.

Now try this

Trevon has a new group of friends, all heavy drinkers. They go drinking and dancing every night, and Trevon is having a great time. He is frequently hungover in the morning but feels better when he starts drinking again the next evening.

Explain Trevon's behaviour, using theories from the learning approach.

 Link your answer to Trevon's behaviour in relation to positive and negative reinforcement, and role models.

Cognitive approach to gambling

The **cognitive** approach can explain **behavioural addictions** such as gambling. Behavioural addictions are **compulsions** (irresistible urges) to participate in non-drug related behaviours that can be rewarding, despite negative consequences for well-being. The cognitive approach to gambling suggests the cause of the addiction is based on irrational and illogical thought processes.

 Expectancy theory

Expectancy theory describes how an addictive behaviour is chosen over a healthier action due to the individual's irrational expectations of the outcomes. Addicts weigh up the pros and cons of their addictive behaviour (e.g. gambling), and think they outweigh pros and cons of the healthy alternative, not gambling.

Real world An addict might think that not gambling makes them boring, so will keep on gambling to remain exciting and popular.

 The Griffiths study (1994)

In **'The role of cognitive bias and skill in fruit machine gambling'**:

- The **aim** was to investigate cognitive bias in regular and non-regular gamblers.

- In the **method**, participants were given £3 to play a fruit machine in a real-life arcade for 60 gambles, aiming to win back the original stake. On reaching 60 plays, they could take the money or keep gambling. Half were asked to say their thoughts aloud.

- In the **findings**, regular gamblers made more irrational comments (cognitive bias) than non-gamblers and believed they were skilful. Successful regular gamblers were also more likely to keep gambling after 60 plays.

Evaluating the approach

Strengths
Griffiths (1994) suggests **cognitive bias**, as shown when thinking aloud, is used when gambling. In rehabilitation, these cognitive biases are **changed** through CBT.
High ecological validity, taking place in real-life arcade.

Weaknesses
Giving money to non-regular gamblers could be an ethical issue, encouraging gambling.
Giving The approach doesn't consider **biological explanations**, such as a genetic predisposition.

① Initiation

Gambling starts when the cost–benefit analysis weighs in gambling's favour. For example, costs and benefits might be:

👍 I feel a thrill when I gamble and win.
👎 I fight with my family when I gamble.
👍 I would save money if I didn't gamble.
👎 I would find it hard to stop gambling.

Gamblers have cognitive biases which:

- suggest they are likely to win
- lead them to overestimate their winnings
- make them underestimate their losses.

② Maintenance

Irrational thoughts play a part in the continuation of gambling behaviour.

- **Cognitive bias** leads addicts to think superstitious behaviours, such as wearing lucky socks, affect outcomes.
- Gamblers **exaggerate their ability** to influence outcomes and win.
- **Illusion of control** is the belief that an individual can use their skill to influence an outcome that is not within their control.

 People who gamble on fruit machines may believe they have a successful technique, but their success is random.

③ Relapse

Recall bias is the tendency to remember and **overestimate success**, and to forget or explain away losses. If winning incentivises gambling and losing doesn't discourage it, relapse is more likely. The gambler falsely believes they will eventually be rewarded, so continues to gamble.

Now try this

Doug plays fruit machines regularly. He says he can 'think himself into being lucky', and that he wins more if he plays the machines in a set order.

Outline the cognitive approach explanation of Doug's gambling behaviour.

89

Learning approach to gambling

Learning approaches suggest that gambling behaviour is acquired through reinforcement and rewards, such as money or prizes from wins. Social learning theory would explain this behaviour through people observing and imitating others who are role models.

1 Initiation

The learning approach can explain the initiation of gambling behaviour. For example:

- When a gambler wins, their behaviour is reinforced (operant conditioning), increasing the likelihood that they will repeat it.
- Gamblers find gambling **exciting**, and this association strengthens their behaviour (classical conditioning).
- If a potential gambler sees adults or role models winning, they may be **vicariously reinforced** and start gambling themselves (social learning theory).

2 Maintenance

Gambling behaviour continues despite making losses, due to the **variable reinforcement schedule** – the reward is given quite frequently but after a variable number of responses.

 Fruit machines pay out using this principle. Since the number of responses (plays) required for a win is unpredictable, this kind of reinforcement strengthens addiction as the next play may win.

Reinforcement schedules

The different forms of reinforcement schedule are: continuous, fixed interval, variable interval, fixed ratio and variable ratio.

3 Relapse

Environmental factors are key to the success of learning theory and explaining relapse in gambling behaviour. For example, exposure to gambling **cues** may cause relapse. Treatment includes identifying and addressing the gambler's cues.

 The lights and music in an arcade may result in **cue reactivity** for fruit-machine addicts. Behavioural cues such as walking past a betting shop or seeing adverts for websites might be reactive for some betting addicts. An emotional state of mind can also trigger an addict's addictive behaviour.

Many people place bets just once a year on the Grand National horse race but do not become addicted to gambling.

Evaluating the approach

Strengths
Evidence supports the learning approach explanations, though generalisability is limited, as sample sizes are limited or only focus on one type of gambling.

Weaknesses
It doesn't explain why many people who gamble do not become addicted, or consider biological approaches to gambling, such as genetic inheritance.
Operant conditioning doesn't explain why gambling behaviour continues even when people continually lose.
It is difficult to apply the learning approach concepts of reinforcement and punishment to types of gambling requiring higher skill levels, such as poker card games.

Now try this

Aki has started playing on the fruit machines during his break at the bowling alley where he works.

Outline how Aki could become addicted to gambling, using the principle of reinforcement schedules.

 Remember that fruit machines pay out quite often but randomly.

Learning approach to shopping

The **learning** approach suggests that people learn from interaction with the environment and by imitating role models. People who wear fashionable clothes and drive the best cars are rewarded and positively reinforced in society. This explains aspects of shopping addiction.

Types of shopping addiction

There are two types of shopping addiction:

- **Impulsive shopping** is making unplanned purchases due to sudden desire for an item.
- **Compulsive shopping** is pre-planned and carried out to escape negative feelings.

Effects of shopping addiction

Shopping can boost self-esteem and make the purchaser feel good. However, it can have similar effects to substance addiction, including undermining trust with significant others and causing relationship breakdown.

❶ Initiation

Shopping addiction starts easily. Ease of credit and online shopping contributes to shopping initiation.

- **Role models** can influence shopping behaviour, as purchasers aspire to be like them, as suggested by social learning theory. Many companies use **celebrity** role models in adverts to promote their products. Adverts show celebrities being reinforced for product use, giving shoppers **vicarious reinforcement**.
- Shopping can be reinforced by rewards (operant conditioning) such as compliments on purchases.
- Shopping can become associated with increased mood (classical conditioning). It may allow the addict to avoid negative feelings and feel in control when in reality they are not.

Social media

Lifestyle role models on social media influence shopping behaviour. People crave the esteem achieved by these role models through 'followers' and 'likes', and make purchases to be like them.

❷ Maintenance

Concepts from the learning approach explain why addicts continue to shop. For example:

- They can experience the reward of an **adrenaline rush** when they decide to buy a product, similar to that of an alcohol or drug addict when they take a substance.
- When in a favourite shop or website, an addict's body releases dopamine, exciting the brain's reward pathway.
- For some addicts, getting sale bargains or obtaining a rare or exclusive item provides **positive reinforcement**.

❸ Relapse

Relapses in shopping behaviour can be explained by the learning approach. For example:

- Shopping is part of everyday life and continual environmental **cues** such as shop windows and **adverts** are difficult to avoid and can trigger the addict's behaviour and need to shop.
- **Negative reinforcement** can occur during withdrawal from shopping. **Withdrawal symptoms** are anxiety and depression. A return to shopping is negatively reinforcing as the withdrawal symptoms diminish.

Evaluating the learning approach to explaining behaviour

Strengths	Weaknesses
👍 The approach explains the role of other people in addictive shopping behaviour and uses therapies such as CBT to treat the addict's thoughts and behaviours.	👎 Doesn't take account of the role biology may take in behavioural addiction.

Now try this

Kev is addicted to shopping and loves sports gear. A basketball player he admires has become the ambassador for a new sportswear brand.

Using principles from the learning approach, suggest a reason why Kev's shopping behaviour could get worse.

This question is about the influence of role models in shopping addiction.

Cognitive approach to shopping

The **cognitive** approach explains shopping addiction in terms of how people think about making purchases. They may have cognitive biases that distort their thinking and behaviour.

Self-medication

Individuals who have **psychological problems**, such as anxiety and depression, may use shopping to make themselves feel better. Some people believe that shopping has important positive effects on them.

Self-medication through shopping regulates mood by distracting from problems.

① Initiation

The self-medication model suggests that initiation of shopping addiction occurs for several reasons. The rational thought-process of shopping in terms of budget is replaced by irrational thinking that purchases will solve problems.

- Shopping addiction can start if the individual expects a behaviour to have a positive outcome, such as **relief of boredom**.
- If they buy products that make them look attractive, people may believe that shopping improves their **self-esteem**.
- Shopping can be a **coping strategy** for **distress** caused by aspects of an individual's work or home life.
- **Excitement** can drive a shopping addiction, especially if the person is driven to find a bargain.

② Maintenance

Cognitive bias explains why people continue to shop, as they think it is helping them, even if in debt.

- When shopping, addicts do not think about the money they are spending.
- They believe that shopping **reduces anxiety and boredom**. However, their stress increases with the financial consequences.
- Some people know their shopping has negative financial consequences but falsely believe they can control their behaviour.
- Some people feel guilty and disappointed after shopping. More shopping makes them feel better again.

③ Relapse

The self-medication model explains reasons for relapse.

- **Withdrawal** from shopping leads to **boredom**. Resuming shopping is **exciting**.
- A relapsing shopper feels anxious before purchasing but knows they will feel better afterwards, so are driven to resume shopping.
- If a person has got into **debt** through shopping, they may experience **anxiety**. This is relieved by relapsing.
- **Coping strategies** may break down if the person feels overwhelmed by their life issues.

Evaluating the approach

Strengths
The approach explains how distorted thinking and behaviour may result in people getting into debt due to shopping addiction, to the extent of losing their home.

Weaknesses
👎 It can be challenging to establish cause and effect for shopping behaviour, which means we do not know whether anxiety/need for excitement has caused the shopping addiction or whether it is a consequence of it.
👎 It does not consider possible biological or genetic explanations for the addiction.

Now try this

Holly experienced depression after she separated from her partner. Now she is shopping every weekend and is getting into debt. Holly says she can give up shopping any time she chooses, but has not actually done so.

Explain, using concepts from cognitive psychology, why Holly may be showing signs of a shopping addiction.

As the question refers to **concepts**, you should consider at least two ideas from the cognitive approach.

Hovland–Yale theory of persuasion

 Key theory The **Hovland–Yale theory of persuasion** (1951) predicts how people change their attitudes and behaviour in response to a **message**.

The process of persuasion

Persuasion can be defined as a process which intentionally influences a person's choice of behaviours or attitudes. Hovland originally devised his theory in relation to US propaganda in the Second World War. The theory suggests that **four** factors persuade an individual to change attitude and behaviour in a sequence of stages, which can be applied in many contexts.

① Communicator

The characteristics of the communicator (the person persuading and the **source** of the message) affect the recipient (the person being persuaded).

- **Personal qualities**, such as expertise, experience, trustworthiness, power and attractiveness, are all persuasive.
- The **use of key figures**, such as medical professionals and celebrities, to support campaigns is effective.

 Real world TV presenter Jeremy Kyle fronted Stoptober 2018 (he quit smoking for a month), and actors Will Ferrell and John C. Reilly promoted Movember 2018 (raising awareness of men's health issues by growing moustaches), with help from Sony Pictures.

② Recipient

The characteristics of the recipient (the **audience**) affect their response to persuasion.

Characteristics include:

- **gender, age** and **cultural background**
- **IQ, personality** and **self-esteem**
- their **processing stages** (the amount of attention paid to the message, the extent to which the communication is understood, the acceptance of information presented, and the amount of the message remembered)
- their **need for cognition** (ability to process and understand information).

 Real world Some people are more influenced by detailed thinking about the message, while others are more influenced by simple cues in publicity.

③ Communication

The communication (content of the message) affects the recipient.

- **Emotional messages** and **fear appeals** influence and persuade people.
- Repetition of the message is helpful.
- Messages with two parts are more effective than single messages.

 Real world Research found that teenagers who were exposed to high threat messages such as 'tobacco use can make you impotent' found it easier to avoid tobacco.

④ Credibility

The credibility (quality) of the source affects the recipient.

- **Highly credibility sources** with evidence, such as experts and trustworthy journals, have a greater persuasive impact compared to low credibility non-expert sources.
- **Well-liked celebrities** can persuade members of the public to buy products.

 Real world *The Lancet* is a highly credible, peer-reviewed medical journal, so its messages are medically persuasive.

Now try this

Franca is a member of the college council, which has decided to do more to reduce plastic waste on campus. The principal has asked Franca to devise and communicate a programme to encourage learners to reduce plastic use and recycle plastic waste.

Using the Hovland–Yale theory, describe how Franca could put forward the council's programme to learners.

Hovland–Yale application

The Hovland–Yale theory can be applied to different contexts and be effective in predicting the influence of persuasion. The **Hovland and Weiss study (1951)** examined the influence of source credibility over time.

Application of the theory

The process of persuasion is effective in these fields:

- **Advertising** – creating **positive emotions** in consumers enhances the promotional message. Products shown in adverts with likeable music are more attractive to consumers than those shown in identical adverts with unpopular music, making them more persuasive.

- **Health promotion** – a **balanced message** with two arguments is more effective in changing teeth-cleaning behaviour than a single argument.

Real world Fear appeals, such as pictures on cigarette packets, have been found to reduce people's desire for certain brands.

Effectiveness in predicting persuasion

👍 Credible sources can be effective in influencing, even when there is a discrepancy between audience beliefs and the message.

👍 Recipients' cognitive processes (page 92) influence their understanding of the message.

👍 Fear appeals can work, especially if information to manage the situation is given.

👎 Effectiveness of communication depends on a popular or attractive communicator.

👎 A campaign will fail if the celebrity is remembered and the message is forgotten.

👎 We can be desensitised to fear appeals.

👎 It ignores the role of cognitive dissonance (contradictory beliefs) in decision-making.

Evaluating the theory

Strengths	Weaknesses
👍 It has informed other research, such as the elaboration-likelihood model (see page 96).	👎 It does not assess whether all four factors are equally important.
👍 It can be used to explain attitude change, through advertising for example.	👎 It identifies persuasive factors, but not how persuasion occurs in the recipient.

🔍 Key study The Hovland and Weiss Study (1951)

In **'The influence of source credibility on communication effectiveness'** study, the **aim** was to examine whether credibility of a source influenced persuasion and if the effect was long-lasting.

- The **method** compared the persuasiveness of a highly credible and a less credible source. Questionnaires tested opinions of Yale students before and after message delivery, and four weeks later.

- The **conclusion** was that credibility mattered initially, but long-term opinion change was the same irrespective of source credibility.

Real world For long-term health change, the persuasive message is more important than the credibility of the source.

- The **findings** showed credible sources were more persuasive. Yet, over time, people forgot the source (sleeper effect), and were less persuaded by the credible source and more persuaded by the less credible source.

Evaluating the study

Strengths	Weaknesses
👍 The study was well controlled so reliable, and has practical application in persuasion.	👎 The study and student sample may be of their time and would not generalise to a wider population.

Now try this

In a vaccination campaign, an eminent doctor uses a fear appeal about the dangers of a childhood illness to deliver a complex message to parents, suggesting they should choose vaccination for their children.

Suggest how the Hovland–Yale theory could predict the success of this health promotion campaign.

Link the four factors of the Hovland–Yale theory (see page 93) to the scenario.

The fear arousal theory

Key theory The fear arousal theory explains the role of fear in promoting positive behavioural change. **Janis and Feshbach's (1953) study** provides evidence to help explain the persuasive impact of different levels of fear on why individuals change their actions.

Key concepts

Fear causes change in attitude and behaviour.

- A person can be scared into listening to, understanding and remembering a message.
- Some people can go through this process and **not** act on the message. If fearful, some may criticise the message rather than change.
- A **fear appeal** creates **fear arousal**. This increases cognitive (thoughts), affective (emotions) and behavioural responses.
- When someone responds to a fear appeal, they reduce the threat or the fear.

Arousal and impact on behaviour

People experience different levels of arousal.

- A **low level** of arousal may create a feeling of boredom so some seek risky activitiies.
- An appropriate or **medium level** of arousal motivates behavioural change.
- A **high level** of arousal can lead to a defensive response or **denial**.

Real world Denial can be common in those most susceptible to the threat, such as heavy smokers or drinkers who may think that cancer or liver disease won't happen to them.

Evaluating strengths and weaknesses of the theory

Strengths	Weaknesses
👍 A Canadian study in 2003 showed that fear images on cigarette packets work better than text.	👎 It is not the only model to explain persuasion and other factors should be considered.

Key study Janis and Feshbach (1953)

In **'Effects of fear-arousing communications'**:

- The **aim** was to investigate the effects of fear appeals on dental hygiene behaviour.
- In the **method**, as part of dental hygiene education, learners in different groups were given examples of diseased mouths, creating different levels of fear arousal.

- In the **findings**, fear arousal didn't affect knowledge about dental hygiene. The minimal and moderate fear arousal groups showed a higher increase in hygiene than the high-fear groups.
- The study **concluded** that the effectiveness of health promotion is reduced by strong fear appeal.

Application

The fear arousal theory has direct application to health education campaigns.

- Janis and Feshbach showed that **medium fear arousal** changes behaviour more than extreme fear.
- Fear arousal is **effective** in campaigns that show desired behaviour, with the level of fear tailored to the audience.

- There are **gender differences** in reaction to fear arousal.
- If an individual is **over aroused** by the message, they may claim it does not apply to them **(denial)**.

Females tend to respond to fear appeals about health; males if sexual performance may be limited.

Habitual drunk drivers may respond to high fear-arousal campaigns by suggesting alcohol doesn't affect their driving skill.

Evaluating strengths and weaknesses of the study

Strengths	Weaknesses
👍 The study was well controlled so reliable, with practical application for effective fear appeals.	👎 The study and sample may not generalise to a wider population or range of health issues.

Now try this

Describe the fear arousal approach to behavioural change, using picture warnings as an example.

Elaboration-likelihood model

 The **elaboration-likelihood model of persuasion** describes how **information processing** brings about **change in attitude**. This requires **elaboration** of the message (effort to understand, evaluate and accept or reject the content) by the recipient. The Petty et al. study (1981) relates to **personal involvement**.

Key concepts

The elaboration-likelihood model describes two main routes to change in attitude.

1 **Central (high) route to persuasion** – the recipient is motivated to give thoughtful consideration to the message.

 Personal relevance of the message is important. When personally affected by a message, we think more about it.

2 **Peripheral (low) route to persuasion** – the recipient is persuaded by positive or negative cues in the message but lacks the ability or motivation to think about the detail.

 This is used when the message is boring or the recipient is distracted.

 ## Application of model

The model has practical application to:

- **health promotion campaigns** – a strong argument for behavioural change is persuasive for people who are personally affected.

- **advertising** – **factors of influence** such as recognising **celebrities** taps into the **central** and **peripheral** routes to persuasion, and increases motivation to process the message.

Effectiveness in predicting change

The theory recognises that a message can be interpreted differently by individuals, using different processes, to give varying levels of persuasion. Individuals differ in their **need for cognition** (see page 92). Some people seek and reflect on information. Others do not analyse the message but rely on the credibility of the source.

Evaluating the model

Strengths	Weaknesses
👍 The theory uses thinking to explain attitude change, rather than punishment or reward.	👎 It is simplistic to use two alternative forms of processing – people may use aspects of both.
👍 It recognises differences in how individuals respond to messages, so has high applicability.	👎 The theory doesn't address temporary attitude change.

 ## Petty et al. (1981)

In **'Personal involvement as a determinant of argument-based persuasion'**:

- The **method** was to see how personal relevance relates to routes of persuasion.

- In the **method**, students rated a message about a new exam. Strong and weak arguments, and expert and non-expert sources were compared. Personal relevance was tested by the new exam starting before (more relevant) or after (less relevant) graduation.

- The **findings** were that the argument's strength **(the central route)** is more important in persuading people to whom the message is personally relevant. **Peripheral cues** are more important as personal involvement decreases.

- The **conclusion** was that people engaged with the message if personally important, or if not, based their attitude on source expertise.

 ## Application of study

Health promotions can use messages tailored for personal involvement to alter behaviour.

Evaluating the study

Strengths
Standardised procedure used for validity.

Weaknesses
It may not generalise to a wider population.

Now try this

Neelam gambled regularly but stopped after carefully considering the message in an online campaign. State which route to persuasion influenced Neelam.

Stress management 1

Treatment and management of stress include **physiological methods** (below) and psychological methods (see page 98). You need to show knowledge and understanding of their effectiveness and ethical and practical factors, apply them to scenarios and justify decisions.

Types of stress

- **Physiological stress** is the body's biological response, for example increased blood pressure, to a stressor.
- **Psychological stress** is the emotional reaction, such as overwhelming anxiety, to a stressor.

Stress management techniques

Stress management techniques aim to:
- reduce a person's stress
- give the person a feeling of control
- improve daily functioning
- promote well-being.

Drug therapy

Drugs are a **biological approach** to managing stress. Drug treatments control the alarm stage of the stress response (page 75) by changing the body's chemistry.

- **Benzodiazepines** (BZs) are anti-anxiety medications, known as tranquilisers. Examples are Valium or Librium. BZs increase the action of the neurotransmitter GABA (gamma-aminobutyric acid) in the body, that acts to reduce the activity of other neurotransmitters in the brain, thus reducing arousal, anxiety and insomnia. It is possible to become addicted to them.

Real world To stop patients becoming reliant on drugs like BZs, a supply of a month at a time is prescribed. The dosage is gradually reduced to manage withdrawal symptoms.

- **Beta blockers** such as propranolol reduce physiological arousal, and stabilise the heart rate and blood pressure by blocking the action of adrenaline. They act fast with fewer side effects than BZs, but may not suit everyone.

Biofeedback

Biofeedback is another **biological approach** that aims to give the stressed person a greater awareness of their body's physical and mental processes using electronic monitoring. This approach involves time and commitment.

- **Physiological feedback** uses technology to measure body functions such as brain waves, heart rate, muscle activity and skin responses. These physiological measures change when the body is faced with stress triggers. When a physiological measure reaches a certain level, an alarm sounds or an indicator light is displayed. The person then uses relaxation strategies to reduce the effects of the stressor.
- **Relaxation training** uses techniques such as meditation, progressive muscle relaxation, visualisation, massage and yoga to reduce the effects of stress. During relaxation heart rate slows down, muscles relax and blood flow to the brain increases.

Ethics

Patients must be informed of potential side effects, including addiction and withdrawal symptoms, of possible treatments.

Many people with stressful jobs attend yoga to allow their brains and bodies to relax, and to aid sleep.

Now try this

Jo is very stressed about her driving lessons and test. She knows this is a short-term situation and would prefer not to use a drug treatment.

Describe a suitable physiological stress management technique for Jo.

To evaluate stress treatments, see page 98.

Stress management 2

Treatment and management of stress includes **psychological methods** (below) and physiological methods (see page 97). You need to show knowledge and understanding of their effectiveness and ethical and practical factors, apply them to scenarios and justify decisions.

Stress inoculation treatment (SIT)

SIT is a **cognitive behavioural treatment** that is carried out with a therapist and has three stages:

1 **Cognitive preparation** – the therapist uses a cognitive interview to identify the nature of the stress. They explain how the treatment works and describe the possible benefits.

2 **Skill acquisition** – the therapist helps the individual learn **coping strategies** (skills such as relaxation techniques) for dealing with stressful situations in the real world.

3 **Application and follow-through** – the patient is gradually exposed to stressors and puts into practice what they have learned. The therapist continues to assist the patient to identify and develop the most successful coping strategies, 'inoculating' against stress.

Social support

Social support for stress management is a structured method, often led by a mental health professional and including family and friends, that offers three forms of support:

1 **instrumental** support (practical help)

Real world Family members may help a relative who has lost their job by loaning them money.

2 **emotional** support (offering comfort)

Real world A friend may talk with a person who has been diagnosed with cancer.

3 **esteem** support (boosting someone's self-belief)

Real world A therapist encourages a gambling addict to develop the confidence to quit.

Real world **An example stress inoculation process**

A therapist and client work together to reduce stress before the client's job interview.

☑ Cognitive preparation (identify cause of stress): job interviews

☑ Skill acquisition (learn coping strategies): relaxation techniques and interview preparation

☑ Application (exposure to stressor): practise job interviews and finally a real interview.

Evaluating treatments

Technique	Effectiveness	Ethics	Practicalities
Drug therapy (page 97)	Manages symptoms of stress rather than addressing cause	Can be addictive	May have side effects
Biofeedback (page 97)	Especially useful with young children; can be applied in everyday life.	Client has control over their therapy	Expensive equipment required; time-consuming
Stress inoculation treatment	Addresses causes of stress, not just the symptoms (long-term solution)	No side effects and no withdrawal symptoms	Requires investment of time (and money) compared to drug therapies
Social support	Research shows it boosts the immune system though it may not provide a long-term solution	Not everybody wants to share their problems	Requires honesty and openness which some may find difficult

---

Now try this

Kirra needs to manage her work stress.

Explain **one** physiological and **one** psychological treatment that Kirra could use.

Addiction treatments 1

Treatment and management of addiction includes **physiological methods** (below) and psychological methods (page 100). You need to show knowledge and understanding of their effectiveness and ethical and practical factors, apply them to scenarios and justify decisions.

Types of addiction

- In **physiological addiction**, a person can't function normally without the addictive substance. Lack of it causes **withdrawal symptoms.**

   Withdrawal from nicotine causes nausea and sweating.

- **Psychological addiction** is a mental need to use a drug or a compulsion to undertake a behaviour.

   An individual may feel that they cannot relax unless they drink alcohol.

Aims of treatment

Aims of addiction treatment are to:

- achieve sustained abstinence
- reduce the risk of physical and psychological harm
- Improve health and well-being.

   Giving up alcohol lowers the risk of conditions such as cancer and liver disease, and can help in the management of psychological problems such as depression.

Preventing relapse

It is important to ensure that relapse into addiction doesn't happen during rehabilitation. Often a combined approach may be more effective.

- Physiological therapies help prevent relapse.
- Psychological support (page 100) helps addicts manage high-risk situations.

   A support group such as Alcoholics Anonymous can prevent relapse.

Drug therapies

Drug therapies can help detoxify the addict from the addictive substance by replacing the addictive drug, reducing withdrawal symptoms or treating anxiety.

 Methadone can be used to replace heroin. **Nicotine replacement therapy** provides an alternative delivery system for nicotine, to treat withdrawal symptoms and break the habit of smoking cigarettes. **Benzodiazepines** (BZs, page 97) can treat physiological and behavioural addictions, by acting on brain receptors to create a calming effect. BZs may be used during detoxification for alcoholism to reduce anxiety and tremors. Their use is short-term to avoid secondary addiction. Examples are Xanax, Valium or Ativan.

Aversion therapy

Aversion therapy uses the principles of **classical conditioning** to treat substance addictions.

- It involves pairing the unwanted behaviour with an unpleasant consequence, thereby removing the pleasure associated with the addictive substance.

   Emetic drugs, such as disulfiram, cause vomiting when taken alongside alcohol. They disassociate drinking from pleasure and associate it with sickness.

An example of a more everyday experience of aversion therapy would be to deter nail biting. A bitter solution is painted onto nails. The experience of nail biting is paired with the effect of the bitter taste and deters the habit.

Now try this

Shane is an alcoholic. His doctor has suggested that he try aversion therapy with disulfiram.

Consider the benefits and disadvantages of this treatment for Shane.

 Refer to the table on page 100 to help you evaluate this treatment.

Addiction treatments 2

Treatment and management of addiction includes **psychological methods** (below) and physiological methods (page 99). You need to show knowledge and understanding of their effectiveness and ethical and practical factors, apply them to scenarios and justify decisions.

Skills training

Skills training removes the unwanted behaviour and replaces it with an acceptable behaviour by learning new coping skills.

- This may involve learning to interact with friends, family or colleagues in social situations where the addictive substance (for example, alcohol or nicotine) will be present.
- Skills training can decrease relapse rates as skills are long-lasting.
- Recovering addicts are asked to practise their new skills as homework.

 Individuals develop daily routines to avoid high-risk situations and help them recover. For example, a shopping addict may need to plan their day carefully to avoid relapse, such as ordering groceries online rather than going to the store.

Cognitive behavioural therapy (CBT)

CBT can be used for physiological and psychological addictions, and stress management.

- CBT focuses on an individual's thoughts, beliefs and attitudes, and how these affect emotions and behaviours.
- CBT involves working with a therapist in multiple sessions over time to identify and challenge negative and faulty thinking processes, eventually replacing dysfunctional beliefs with positive ones.

 A gambling addict may use the therapy sessions progressively. Initially, they would set out their goals and, subsequently, they may practise coping strategies or address negative and faulty thought processes.

Evaluating treatments

Treatment	Effectiveness	Ethics	Practicalities
Aversion therapy (page 99)	Client may realise that the medication is making them ill and then relapse	Vomiting or pain are distressing, but less harmful than the addictive substance and side effects	Most cases are treated in a residential setting or hospital, which has cost implications
Drug therapy (page 99)	Should only be prescribed for a short period of time to avoid secondary addiction	Can lead to dependency on more than one drug (polydrug use)	Therapeutic drugs can be misused for recreational purposes, or to increase the effect of the addictive drug
CBT	With motivation, can be effective (especially when combined with another treatment)	Client has a high level of control	Requires a qualified practitioner; waiting lists are long. Not available on the NHS for all addictions
Skills training	Homework is crucial to skills training; the client practises new skills in real-life situations	High drop-out rate, so may not be useful in all forms of addiction	Sessions occur over time. Difficult to treat biological aspects of addiction using this approach

Now try this

Billie discusses treatments for drug addiction with his doctor. Evaluate a physiological and a psychological therapy for Billie.

 Refer also to page 99.

Rational non-adherence

Rational non-adherence attempts to explain the reasons why people **deliberately** choose not to maintain advised lifestyle changes, such as taking medication or stopping addictive behaviours.

Adherence and non-adherence

- **Adherence** is following the advice of health professionals. This could involve reducing alcohol intake or taking medication.

- **Non-adherence** is not following a treatment programme. Symptoms of illness may get worse; addictive behaviour may become more extreme.

- **Rational non-adherence** is a **deliberate** choice not to follow medical advice, a decision which the patient believes is justified.

 Reasons given for not complying include disagreeing with the medical diagnosis and fear of side effects.

Financial barriers

The need to invest financially in recovery may lead to non-adherence. Financial barriers to behavioural change can include the cost of treatment which is not provided by the NHS. A long-term stay in a residential facility (rehab) or in hospital may interrupt earnings.

 A financial barrier to treatment could be the cost of travel to hospital for medical appointments.

The patient–practitioner relationship

If an individual does not feel supported by their doctor, they are less likely to comply with medical advice and may relapse into addictive behaviour. In order to increase adherence to treatment programmes, practitioners should:

- nurture positive relationships with patients

- educate patients in what to expect from the treatment programme, including any side effects

- schedule appointments at convenient times.

Cost–benefit analysis

Patients consider the costs and benefits of illness/addiction and treatment.

- If the **cost of treatment** is high, the patient may not adhere to the regime.

- If the **cost of addiction** is high, the patient may stick to the programme.

- There are also **costs of not adhering** to a treatment programme.

 A physical **cost of treatment** could be side effects of medication. An emotional **cost of addiction** might be loss of family support. The **cost of not adhering** to antibiotic treatment is recurrent infection.

Lack of understanding

Patient understanding of medical advice increases adherence. Use of medical jargon leads to non-adherence.

 Treatment for alcoholism can involve aversion therapy whereby medication makes the alcoholic vomit if paired with taking alcohol. In order to comply, the alcoholic must understand how the treatment programme works.

 Key study **Bulpitt and Fletcher (1988)**

In '**Importance of well-being to hypertensive patients**':

- The **aim** was to review research on adherence in high blood pressure treatment.

- In the **method**, articles on the physical and psychological effects of medication, including side effects, were reviewed.

- **Findings** included sleepiness, dizziness, loss of sexual function and impaired cognition.

- **Conclusion:** when the side effects (costs) outweighed the benefits, patients were less likely to comply with treatment.

Evaluating strengths and weaknesses of the study

Strengths	Weaknesses
👍 Supports the cost-benefit analysis.	👎 Depends on validity of research in literature review.

Now try this

Discuss how adherence to a weight-loss programme can be improved.

⬅ Use the principles on this page to guide your answer.

Ley's cognitive model

Key theory Ley's cognitive model (1988) suggests a patient's understanding of their medical condition, memory of and level of satisfaction with the consultation affect **adherence to advice**.

Ley identified three factors that affect whether a patient adheres to medical advice:

- understanding
- memory
- level of satisfaction with medical advice.

Memory aids, such as this pill box, which enables the patient to see whether or not they have taken their daily treatment, can improve adherence.

1 Role of understanding

Lack of understanding can affect a patient's adherence to a treatment programme.

- Doctors may feel they will overwhelm patients if they give them too much information at one appointment.
- Patients don't always understand their medical conditions in detail.
- A great deal of medical information is available online, but can be misleading.

Real world If a GP gives structured information that is not too technical, a patient is more likely to understand what to do.

2 Role of memory

Memory and recall are important for adherence to a treatment programme.

- Half of all information presented in a medical consultation is forgotten.
- If a patient has event-based recall rather than time-based recall, they may be more successful in following their medical regime by taking medication around a meal, for example.

Real world If a GP gives important information first or last it is more likely to be remembered.

3 Role of patient–provider relationship

Ley suggested that having a **satisfactory consultation** with a doctor is central to whether a patient follows medical advice. Effective communication has positive implications for doctor–patient relationships.

Patients look for attributes in their clinicians:

- expert knowledge and lack of bias
- good listening skills and ability to explain clearly.

Real world If a patient sees the same GP for appointments and has time to talk, this can maximise satisfaction and improve adherence.

Effectiveness in predicting change

 Ley's model empowers individuals to take responsibility for their own actions and change behaviour, reducing the effect of the situation.

 Interventions that improve cognitive processing (providing better understanding) lead to more successful treatment.

 The model raises ethical issues as it places great power in the practitioner's hands to identify which aspects of an individual's life are faulty or inappropriate.

Now try this

Jagdeep, a care assistant, knows the importance of understanding, memory and satisfaction for adherence to treatment programmes.

Using Ley's cognitive model, identify why Jagdeep's elderly patients may not follow medical advice.

The question clearly asks you to address all three aspects of Ley's model.

Adherence and physiology

Non-adherence to, or not following, medical advice is a serious problem. You should know and be able to evaluate methods to improve adherence. **Lustman et al. (2000)** used antidepressants to improve adherence to treatment in people with diabetes and depression.

Physiological methods

Physiological methods, such as urine or blood tests, may improve adherence to advice for behavioural change. If people can see the effects of their behavioural change (health improvements), they will feel motivated and are more likely to adhere.

 If someone gives up smoking and there is a decrease in their blood pressure, they can see the health benefit of their behavioural change and are more likely to continue.

Use of antidepressants

Many people who are prescribed antidepressants for depression, obsessive-compulsive disorder (OCD), anxiety and post-traumatic stress disorder (PTSD) do not use their medication correctly. As a result, they don't benefit from the treatment or risk relapse.

 Some people think they no longer need antidepressants once they start to feel better and stop taking them, whereas they should gradually decrease the dose under medical supervision.

 Lustman et al. (2000)

In **'Fluoxetine for depression in diabetes: a randomized double-blind placebo-controlled trial'**:

- The **aim** was to treat depressed diabetic patients with an antidepressant (fluoxetine) to increase their adherence to diabetes treatment and improve their overall health.

- In the **method**, participants with type 1 or type 2 diabetes and a depressive disorder entered into a short-term, double-blind placebo/antidepressant study. Physiological measures (blood tests) were used to measure adherence to a medical regime for diabetes.

- The **findings** were that an antidepressant reduced depression compared to a placebo, and that antidepressant treatment improved diabetic patients' control of blood sugar, indicating better adherence to their medical regime.

- **Conclusion:** Treatment for depression caused by long-term illness can improve patients' management of their condition, leading to better health outcomes.

Evaluating strengths and weaknesses of the study

Strengths	Weaknesses
👍 The study shows that using physiological methods can be effective in behavioural change for diabetes treatment.	👎 The sample was made up of diabetic patients. Findings may not be replicated for other illnesses or behavioural addictions.
👍 In a double-blind procedure, objectivity is increased.	👎 The study was short-term, so the long-term implications of antidepressant treatment for diabetic patients are not known.

Now try this

Moses has type-1 diabetes, which he finds hard to control due to a chaotic lifestyle. Moses's long-term struggle to manage his diabetes leads to frequent bouts of depression.

Suggest how antidepressants could help Moses improve his diabetes management. Refer to the findings of Lustman et al. in your answer.

 This page revises the link between treatment for depression and better management of diabetes.

Adherence and psychology

Psychological methods can improve adherence to medical treatment. **Volpp et al. (2009)** looked at ways to help people stick to a programme for stopping smoking.

Psychological methods to improve adherence

Psychological methods can help people stick to treatment plans for stress and addiction.

These are often used in combination:
- memory aids, reminder calls and texts
- cognitive behavioural therapy (CBT)

- self-reporting
- feedback from health professionals
- family support.

Use of reinforcements

Incentive-based reward schemes can increase adherence to treatment programmes. Using principles from operant conditioning, if an individual is rewarded for desired behaviour they are likely to repeat it. The more frequent the reinforcement, the more likely the behaviour is to be repeated.

Use of financial incentives

Financial incentives may also improve adherence to a treatment programme. High-risk, non-adherent individuals for whom all other incentives have failed may benefit from financial incentives. Financial incentives work best if the reward is given immediately and consistently.

 Key study Volpp et al. (2009)

In 'A randomized, controlled trial of financial incentives for smoking cessation':

- The **aim** was to investigate the effects of financial incentives on cessation of smoking.
- In the **method**, a large sample of participants from one workplace all received the same information about stopping smoking, but some also received a financial incentive of $100–$400.

- In the **findings**, people in the financially incentivised group had higher smoking cessation rates than the information-only group.
- **Conclusion:** financial incentives can significantly help people stop smoking as they positively reinforce behavioural change.

Evaluating strengths and weaknesses of the study

Strengths	Weaknesses
👍 The findings show that incentivised treatment programmes can be effective in changing health-related behaviour.	👎 Incentivised schemes don't address the cause of the problem.
👍 A large sample increases the generalisability of the findings.	👎 Generalising findings to employees from other companies may be problematic.

Now try this

Imran runs a drug treatment centre. He wants to improve attendance at the centre and adherence to treatment programmes.

Using your knowledge of Volpp et al. (2009), suggest how Imran could improve the attendance and adherence for drug addicts.

This question assumes that the findings of Volpp et al. in relation to smoking addiction can be linked to addiction to other substances.

Had a look ☐   Nearly there ☐   Nailed it! ☐

Your Unit 3 exam

Your Unit 3 exam will be set by Pearson and could cover any of the essential content in the unit. You can revise the unit content in this Revision Guide. This skills section is designed to **revise skills** that might be needed in your exam. The section uses selected content and outcomes to provide examples of ways of applying your skills.

Exam checklist

Before your exam, make sure you have:

☑ a black pen you like and at least one spare

☑ double checked the time and date of your exam

☑ a good night's sleep

☑ eaten in a healthy way

☑ water.

Check the Pearson website

The questions and sample response extracts in this section are provided to help you revise content and skills. Ask your tutor or check the Pearson website for the most up-to-date **sample assessment material (SAM)** and **mark scheme** to get an indication of the structure of your actual paper and what this requires of you. The details of the actual exam may change so always make sure you are up to date.

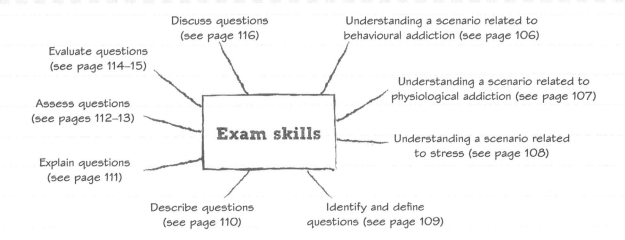

Evaluate questions (see page 114–15)

Discuss questions (see page 116)

Understanding a scenario related to behavioural addiction (see page 106)

Understanding a scenario related to physiological addiction (see page 107)

Assess questions (see pages 112–13)

Exam skills

Understanding a scenario related to stress (see page 108)

Explain questions (see page 111)

Describe questions (see page 110)

Identify and define questions (see page 109)

Understanding and responding to scenarios

Questions will relate to scenarios using different contexts related to **behavioural addiction**, **physiological addiction** and **stress** that give information about a person's realistic situation and context. They will assess your applied knowledge, understanding and critical evaluation of psychological **approaches**, **theories** and **studies** that explain or predict health-related behaviour and **behavioural change**.

Now try this

Visit the Pearson website and find the page containing the course materials for BTEC National Applied Psychology. Look at the latest Unit 3 SAM for an indication of:

- the paper you have to take
- whether the paper is in sections
- how much time is allowed and how many marks are allocated
- what types of questions appear on the paper.

Your tutor or teacher may already have provided you with a copy of the SAM. You can use it as a 'mock' exam to practise before taking your actual exam.

Understanding scenarios 1

When reading a scenario relating to **behavioural addiction** and answering questions based on it, you will need to apply your knowledge of health psychology to **gambling** or **shopping**.

Here is an example scenario based on shopping. The comments help you consider ways that your knowledge of health psychology could be applied. In your exam, you will apply your knowledge in response to the focus of the questions. **Questions in this skills section relate to this scenario.**

Anita is a 30-year-old female who <u>enjoys looking her best</u>. She is a partner in a successful interior design company. Her success is important to her as in the past she had <u>low self-esteem, social anxiety and depression, and sometimes still does.</u>

Read a scenario carefully and consider ways to explain behavioural addiction. You could identify significant elements in the scenario by underlining them, as shown here.

Anita often takes clients to high-end furniture stores and <u>dresses appropriately</u> for these environments. <u>She has observed</u> that many successful people in her industry dress well and she <u>aspires to be like them</u>. Anita has also strengthened her <u>professional profile online,</u> uploading regular images of the designs she has created. This has involved buying new products. When <u>likes</u> and <u>positive comments</u> are made in response, she feels an <u>increase in self-esteem.</u>

Consider reasons suggested in the individual's background for the initiation and maintenance of addiction. For this **shopping** scenario, you could apply the learning approach and cognitive approach (such as self-medication). If a gambling scenario, you could consider the learning approach and cognitive approach (such as expectancy theory).

Her business partner, Sam, has recently noticed that Anita is <u>spending more money on outfits</u> to meet with clients, and on designer products. Sam is <u>worried that Anita is taking too much money out of the business</u>. When asked about this, Anita told Sam <u>not to worry and there wasn't a problem</u>. She said she just needed a few new things and she was in control of her spending.

Think about theories and studies that might apply. For example, health belief model, locus of control, planned behaviour, self-efficacy.

Anita's friends were also concerned, so met her in places <u>other than shopping centres</u> to encourage her to spend less. However, Anita then started to visit <u>online auction sites to try to get the best deals, but she kept this secret.</u>

Consider physiological and psychological impact of behaviour, and positive reinforcement. Here, for example, there is an adrenaline rush from excitement at getting the best deals on purchases.

If Anita keeps taking money from the business to <u>spend on clothes and products, there is a danger that she will place the business at financial risk.</u> She doesn't like to think about money and <u>won't admit that there is a problem</u> but, after an argument with Sam, <u>Anita agrees to reduce her spending.</u>

Think about risks of maintaining an addiction. Here, for example, you could consider the effect of cognitive bias in knowing the negative financial consequences but falsely believing the behaviour is under control.

Anita reads an article about someone in her industry who had a problem with spending, and learns that <u>cognitive behavioural therapy (CBT) or skills training</u> can be used to change an individual's relationship with shopping. Anita decides to look into this.

Consider promotion of positive behavioural change in relation to theories of persuasion, treatment and management, and maintenance of behavioural change.

Now try this

Identify **two** examples from the scenario that suggest Anita is addicted to shopping.

Links To revise behavioural addiction and shopping, see the learning approach (page 91) and the cognitive approach (page 92).

Understanding scenarios 2

When reading a scenario relating to **physiological addiction** and answering questions based on it, you will need to apply your knowledge of health psychology to **smoking** or **alcohol**.

Here is an example scenario based on alcohol. The comments help you consider ways that your knowledge of health psychology could be applied. In your exam, you will apply your knowledge in response to the focus of the questions. **Questions in this skills section relate to this scenario.**

Stacey is 20 years old and works in a high-pressure telephone-sales office. After her mother's death when Stacey was 18, <u>she and her father started drinking alcohol together to take the edge off their loss and help them deal with their emotions. They gradually became more dependent on alcohol to get them through this time.</u>

Read a scenario carefully and consider ways to explain physiological addiction. You could identify significant elements in the scenario by underlining them, as shown here.

Stacey did <u>try to give up alcohol</u>, but her <u>friends like to have a drink and she found herself joining in with them to be sociable.</u> Now the pressure of her work means she is <u>drinking in the day as well as the evenings.</u> At first it helped with the <u>stress and made her feel relaxed.</u> However, due to her drinking, she is finding it increasingly <u>difficult to get out of bed for work.</u> Her employers have tried to be supportive but <u>she is now on her third and final warning and is in danger of losing her job.</u> She <u>feels detached</u> if she doesn't have another drink to make her <u>feel like herself again.</u> She is drinking <u>more and more</u> in order to get the <u>same feelings of relaxation.</u>

Consider reasons suggested in the individual's background for the initiation and maintenance of addiction. For this **alcohol** scenario, you could apply the cognitive approach (such as self-medication model) and the learning approach (such as operant conditioning).

Stacey understands that her <u>behaviour is a problem</u> as she has <u>lost weight</u> due to not eating. She also experiences <u>high levels of anxiety when she hasn't had a drink</u> and feels <u>depressed.</u> Stacey realises that <u>she must give up alcohol or she will lose her job, but she can no longer get through the day without drinking.</u> When she is with friends it makes her feel more <u>sociable and outgoing.</u>

Consider how the initiation and maintenance of addiction can be explained – here, for example, you could consider the roles of self-medication, and positive and negative reinforcement. Think about the escalation of drinking to achieve self-medication, and the desire to avoid negative experiences and seek relaxation.

Consider theories and studies that might apply. For example, health belief model, locus of control, planned behaviour, self-efficacy. Think about the physiological and psychological impact of behaviour.

Stacey booked an <u>appointment with her GP</u> to discuss <u>treatments or therapies available to help her to change her behaviour.</u> She tells the GP she is <u>desperate and will do anything to give up alcohol.</u> The GP provides Stacey with information about different methods that could help her quit alcohol for good, including CBT from a <u>cognitive perspective,</u> to help her <u>change her thinking patterns about and emotional responses</u> to drinking, and <u>aversion therapy</u> from the <u>learning approach.</u>

Think about the risks of maintaining addiction. Consider the promotion of positive behavioural change in relation to theories of persuasion, treatment and management, and maintenance of behavioural change.

Now try this

Explain how the treatment of aversion therapy would help Stacey change her behaviour.

Make sure you clearly link your explanation with the scenario.

Links To revise addiction treatments, see pages 99–100.

Understanding scenarios 3

When reading a scenario relating to **stress** and answering questions based on it, you will need to apply your knowledge of health psychology to stress.

Here is an example scenario. The comments help you consider ways that your knowledge of health psychology could be applied. In your exam, you will apply your knowledge in response to the focus of the questions. **Questions in this skills section relate to this scenario.**

Malik is 55 years old and married with two grown-up daughters. He is a team leader on <u>a production line in a chemical factory</u>, and has additional <u>responsibility for the health and safety of his team</u>. The environment is pressured, as health and safety regulations are important in such situations of <u>high demand</u> and <u>repetitive tasks</u>, in order to safeguard against harmful substances.

Read a scenario carefully and consider ways to explain stress. You could identify significant elements in the scenario by underlining them, as shown here.

Malik and his wife are selling <u>their family house and downsizing to a smaller home to help</u> one daughter <u>pay for her wedding</u> and the other <u>buy her first house</u>. Malik's <u>closest friend</u> has suddenly died, and Malik is <u>responsible for carrying out instructions in his friend's will, including selling his house</u>. His <u>computer keeps crashing</u> so everything is <u>taking longer</u>.

Consider reasons suggested for the causes of stress – here for example, you could consider effect of life changes and daily hassles. Think about physiological and psychological stress, perceived ability to cope, and the difference between chronic and acute stress.

Malik was present during a chemical accident at work in which a <u>member of his team was hurt</u>. The factory had recently implemented a <u>new shift pattern with additional hours</u> to cope with increased demand. Malik <u>advised management</u> on the risks of the change in shifts in pressured and repetitive conditions, but <u>feels they didn't properly listen</u>. He was required to <u>implement the new shift pattern</u> for his team <u>even though he was concerned about the risks</u>, and now he has also been asked to investigate the accident.

Think about whether the workplace has a role in an individual's stress.

Consider theories and studies that might apply. For example, health belief model, locus of control, planned behaviour, self-efficacy.

For some time, Malik has <u>shown symptoms of stress and is feeling increasingly unwell</u>. He has become <u>irritable</u> with his family and shuts himself away. He is especially <u>anxious</u> when leaving for work. One morning, he cannot find his car keys. He notices his <u>breathing and heart rate become much faster than normal and feels dizzy</u>, not for the first time. His wife is worried as, in addition, Malik's <u>sleeping patterns are disturbed</u>, so he paces around the house in the night.

Consider the physiological and psychological response to chronic and acute stress, including links between stress and ill health, and impact on the immune and cardiac systems.

Malik has considered seeing a therapist but is worried about the commitment that treatment, such as <u>stress inoculation treatment (SIT)</u>, <u>requires</u>.

Think about the risks associated with stress. Consider the promotion of positive behavioural change in relation to theories of persuasion, treatment and management, and maintenance of behavioural change.

Now try this

Explain how stress caused by the life changes and daily hassles in the scenario might affect Malik's health.

Make sure you clearly link your explanation with the scenario.

Links To revise causes and effects of stress, see pages 72–73.

Identify and define questions

If you are asked an **identify** question, you need to select some key information from the scenario provided. If you are asked a **define** question you need to state the meaning of something using the correct terms. These questions require short answers with limited development.

Worked example

Identify the effect on Anita of interest in her social media posts.

Anita has increased self-esteem when she receives a positive comment about her uploads to social media.

 This question relates to the behavioural scenario on page 106. Select Anita's response from the scenario. No further detail is required for an identify question.

Identify **one** reason why Stacey drinks alcohol regularly.

Stacey drinks alcohol regularly to help cope with her emotions following the loss of her mum.

 This question relates to the physiological scenario on page 107. Select one reason from the scenario. No development is required for an identify question.

Identify **two** examples in the scenario that might be causing Malik to be stressed.

1. Malik is downsizing and moving house, suggesting stress as a result of major life changes.
2. Malik was present during a serious incident at work, suggesting stress as a result of his work situation.

 This question relates to the stress scenario on page 108. Select two examples from the scenario.

Define the term addiction in relation to Stacey's signs of addiction in the scenario.

In addiction, an individual develops a biological or psychological dependency on a substance or behaviour, such as Stacey's need for alcohol.

 This question relates to the physiological scenario on page 107. Show you understand a key term or concept by writing enough to make your meaning clear, linking to the scenario where required.

Define the term stressor in relation to Malik's current life experiences.

A stressor is an event or situation that causes the release of stress hormones within the body. Malik's stressors range from daily hassles, such as his computer crashing, to life events, such as the death of his friend.

 This question relates to the stress scenario on page 108. Show you understand a key term or concept by linking it with the scenario where required.

Now try this

Cognitive behavioural therapy (CBT) could help Anita change her addictive behaviour.

Define CBT as a treatment to help Anita change her behaviour.

 This question relates to the behavioural scenario on page 106.

 Links To revise cognitive behavioural therapy, see page 100.

Describe questions

If you are asked a **describe** question, you need to give an account of something. A justification or reason does not need to be included. Make sure that your response gives a clear account of the facts and main features of the theory, study or treatment.

Worked example

Describe how advertisements featuring celebrities might have influenced Anita's behavioural addiction to shopping.

Anita's shopping addiction involves purchasing clothes she thinks she needs to succeed in business. Social learning theory suggests that Anita could be influenced by adverts for clothes featuring celebrities whom she admires as role models and wishes to imitate. Anita may aspire to wear the same clothes as the celebrities, and this will drive her shopping addiction. Vicarious reinforcement will occur when Anita, after observing the celebrities in adverts wearing a particular outfit and receiving compliments, wears the outfit and expects to receive the compliments herself.

 This question relates to the behavioural scenario on page 106. Here, the question requires you to choose the relevant approach in relation to the role of celebrities in advertising, which is the learning approach.

 Consider the key words that are important in your account of the facts and features. For example, when drawing on the learning approaches to behavioural addiction, key words could include role model, or positive and vicarious reinforcement.

Describe why Stacey feels more relaxed when she drinks alcohol.

Alcohol interacts with neurotransmitters in Stacey's brain to give a sedative effect, calming her brain and relaxing her body.

 This question relates to the physiological scenario on page 107. It requires you to describe the physiological effects of drinking alcohol. Make sure you link your account to the scenario where required. Here, knowledge about the effect alcohol has on physiology is linked to Stacey.

Describe the role which adrenaline may have played in Malik's initial response to the accident at work.

The adrenal gland situated within Malik's kidney releases adrenaline as part of the fight-or-flight response to immediate danger and in situations of acute stress. This response is initiated by a sudden stressful situation, such as the accident at work. Malik may have noticed physiological changes in his body, such as a racing heart, fast breathing and sweating. A heightened state of awareness and extra energy may have helped Malik deal with the crisis.

 This question relates to the stress scenario on page 108. Make sure you link your account to the scenario where required. This answer gives an account of where adrenaline is created, the changes it causes in Malik's body and how this affects Malik's response.

Now try this

Describe how Malik could use stress inoculation treatment to treat his stress.

 This question relates to the stress scenario on page 108.

⚭ Links To revise stress inoculation treatment see page 98.

Explain questions

If you are asked an **explain** question, you need to identify a point and then justify it or give a linked example. The answer must contain some linked reasoning. Some explain questions require shorter answers and others longer answers. Here are some examples.

Worked example

The theory of planned behaviour (TPB) describes and predicts addictive behaviour.

Explain how the TPB relates to Anita's shopping addiction.

Anita's personal attitude to shopping is that she buys clothes to look good at work. Her subjective norms are that she thinks Sam is overreacting. Anita's perceived behavioural control is that she thinks she can control her spending. The TPB suggests that Anita is unlikely to change her behaviour in these circumstances.

 This question relates to the behavioural scenario on page 106. It requires you to relate theory to practice. Think about the implications of the theory on behavioural change. If the question asked is in relation to the scenario, make sure your answer relates to the scenario throughout.

There are many reasons why individuals do not adhere to treatment programmes for addictions.

Explain how financial barriers may prevent Stacey from adhering to her treatment programme.

Stacey might not earn a high salary so might not be able to afford residential rehabilitation or to pay for prescriptions. She could relapse due to financial barriers rather than failing to adhere to treatment.

 This question relates to the physiological scenario on page 107. It requires consideration of the financial barriers to maintenance of behavioural change. Think practically about why Stacey might not maintain a treatment programme for her alcoholism.

Explain **one** strength and **one** weakness of using stress inoculation treatment to treat Malik's stress.

Strength: Stress inoculation treatment (SIT) includes learning to apply coping strategies and relaxation techniques. The treatment will help Malik recognise his stressors such as life changes (downsizing), daily hassles (losing keys) and workplace stress, and teach him skills to cope with them. This will give him the capacity to deal with current stressors but also different stressors in the future.

Weakness: Stress inoculation treatment is time-consuming and emotionally demanding, requiring Malik's long-term commitment. He must be completely honest with his therapist and prepared to practise relaxation techniques. The long-term nature of the treatment means that Malik might not see immediate results, so he could become discouraged and less willing to put in the effort required.

 This question relates to the stress scenario on page 108. It requires you to identify an appropriate strength and weakness, and justify each one. Make sure you provide enough relevant detail when answering this kind of question. Link your response to the scenario throughout.

Now try this

 This question relates to the stress scenario on page 108.

Malik has a Type A personality. Explain how Malik's personality type could influence his responses to the stressors in his life.

 Links To revise the role of personality in stress, see page 74.

Assess questions

If you are asked an **assess** question, you need to consider the factors or events that apply to a scenario and identify which are the most important or relevant. You make a judgement on the importance of something, and come to a conclusion.

Qualities when answering an assess question

If asked an **assess** question that requires a longer answer, consider how your response will be balanced and show:

✓ accurate and detailed knowledge and understanding

✓ points that are relevant to the context in the question, with clear links to the scenario

✓ a well-developed and logical assessment that clearly considers the factors or events and their relative importance, leading to a supported conclusion.

Worked example

The learning approach suggests that behaviour is acquired through interacting with the environment and by observing other people.

Assess the effectiveness of the learning approach in explaining Anita's behaviour. You must refer to **one** other approach in your answer.

Sample response extract

The learning approach explains behavioural addiction to shopping in terms of behaviour learned from environmental stimuli and observing and imitating role models (social learning theory). This is effective in explaining Anita's behaviour, along with consideration of the reward element from compliments, for example (operant conditioning) and of the association with improved mood (classical conditioning). However, the cognitive approach also offers a powerful explanation of shopping addiction, focusing on shopping as a form of self-medication for psychological problems, resulting from faulty thinking that shopping is a solution.

The learning approach is effective as it would explain the initiation of Anita's behavioural addiction to shopping. She has observed how successful people in her industry dress. They act as role models for Anita and she aspires to be like them. She buys clothes to imitate the role models and seeks the reward of compliments.

The learning approach is also effective in explaining the maintenance of Anita's shopping addiction. If shopping makes her feel good, she will experience positive reinforcement for her behaviour and is more likely to repeat it. Shopping on online auction sites may be particularly reinforcing as winning items at bargain prices may be very exciting for Anita and there may be an association between excitement and shopping resulting in conditioned response behaviour. Griffiths' components of addiction would support that Anita's addictive behaviour has become a psychological dependence, and suggests that to avoid tolerance, Anita would need increasing amounts of the addictive behaviour to obtain the same physical, psychological or emotional responses.

This question and extract from an example response relates to the behavioural scenario on page 106. You will need to show these qualities if asked an assess question on any scenario. The question expects you to both assess the effectiveness of the learning approach by referring to one other approach **and** show your accurate and detailed knowledge and understanding, linked to the scenario, to explain Anita's behaviour.

You have to make a judgement on whether you think the learning approach is effective in explaining Anita's behaviour.

Give careful consideration to the different factors that apply to Anita's addiction and make a judgement on which are the most relevant. Choose what to focus on in your answer so that you can assess in depth, rather than writing a little about too many things.

Make sure your points are relevant and clearly link to the scenario to explain Anita's behaviour throughout. Remember that only using a name from the scenario in your answer does not count as a link.

Apply your knowledge to show your understanding and support the points you make.

The answer continues on the next page.

Assess questions (continued)

The example **assess question** starts on page 112 and continues below.

The cognitive approach, however, would explain Anita's addiction to shopping in terms of faulty thinking about making purchases, and self-medication. In addicts such as Anita, the normal cognitive process associated with the ordinary behaviour of shopping becomes distorted.

 Show accurate and detailed knowledge using the correct terminology as you assess each approach.

The initiation of Anita's behaviour is explained by the cognitive approach as it proposes shopping as a form of self-medication for relief from her low self-esteem, social anxiety and depression. Shopping will distract Anita from her problems, and positive outcomes will make her feel better and improve her self-esteem.

 Consider the effectiveness of the alternative approach in explaining different stages of addiction.

Anita maintains her addiction as she has a cognitive bias towards her shopping – she believes she has her spending under control. She continues to shop even though it is affecting trusted relationships and may put her business at risk. She does not like to think about money and doesn't acknowledge the negative consequences of spending.

 Show a logical assessment of different factors that are of relevance to the scenario.

The cognitive approach suggests that thinking skills are important in explaining addictive behaviour, whereas the learning approach explains addiction in terms of the external influences of other people and the environment. Rotter's theory of locus of control and his 1996 study would suggest that Anita's thinking shows an external locus of control that is more influenced by external forces, such as role models, and this affects her decisions, her health behaviour and her ability to change. Both approaches have been criticised for not taking into account possible biological and genetic factors in addictive behaviour and personalities.

 You can support your careful consideration of different factors by applying theories and studies.

 Assess the strengths and limitations of both approaches to support your evaluation, so that your judgement is balanced.

Different aspects of Anita's addiction to shopping may be explained effectively by the learning and cognitive approaches. Neither approach is totally effective in explaining all aspects of Anita's shopping addiction. They could be more effective as a treatment for Anita's behaviour if used in combination with each other.

 Make a judgement on the effectiveness of the approaches and come to a conclusion.

Now try this

Outline what you would include in response to the following question, which relates to the stress scenario on page 108.

Malik has agreed to see his GP. The doctor recommends beta blockers and stress inoculation treatment to treat Malik's stress. Assess the effectiveness of the two methods in helping Malik manage his stress levels.

 Links To revise physiological and psychological stress management techniques, see pages 97–98.

Evaluate questions

If you are asked an **evaluate** question, you need to consider various aspects of a subject's qualities in relation to its context, such as strengths and weaknesses, advantages or disadvantages, pros or cons. You should come to a judgement, supported by evidence, which will often be in the form of a conclusion.

Qualities when answering an evaluate question

If asked an **evaluate** question that requires a longer answer, consider how your response will be balanced and show:

☑ accurate and detailed knowledge and understanding

☑ points that are relevant to the context in the question, with clear links with the scenario

☑ a well-developed and logical evaluation that clearly considers different aspects and competing points in detail, leading to a fully supported conclusion.

Worked example

Evaluate **one** physiological treatment that the GP could offer Stacey for treating her addiction.

Sample response extract

Stacey could use aversion therapy to treat her alcohol addiction, as she has said to her GP that she is desperate and will do anything to stop drinking alcohol.

Aversion therapy uses the principles of classical conditioning to treat addiction. Stacey would be prescribed a drug, such as Antabuse (disulfiram) or naltrexone. These drugs cause vomiting when taken with alcohol. Repeated pairings of alcohol and medication would create a negative set of consequences for Stacey, so she would learn to avoid alcohol.

By manipulating the stimulus of the addictive substance, it is possible to be effective in changing Stacey's response to drinking. However, aversion therapy can be quite expensive, especially if Stacey is required to attend a residential facility in the initial stages of her treatment. A disadvantage of this form of medication is that it can cause long-term side effects, such as liver damage, changes to vision and seizures. Because of this, and because vomiting is distressing, it is usually only used as a treatment of last resort in cases of severe addiction and when other therapies have failed. Stacey has indicated that she is desperate to stop drinking alcohol but would need to decide if this treatment is suitable for her situation. Also, the treatment may not be effective if Stacey cannot cope with the distress and how it makes her feel ill. She could relapse if she stops taking her prescribed treatment to avoid the distress of vomiting.

This question and extract from a sample response relates to the physiological scenario on page 107. You may be asked an evaluate question in relation to any given scenario. Link your answer to the scenario throughout.

Introduce the selected therapy, with accurate use of technical and specialist language. Show accurate and detailed knowledge of the therapy, such as its features and how it could be used to treat Stacey's alcohol misuse.

Evaluate the advantages and disadvantages associated with use of the treatment. For example, learning to avoid alcohol is an advantage. Side effects are disadvantages.

The answer continues on the next page.

Evaluate questions (continued)

The example **evaluate question** starts on page 114 and continues below.

Although aversion therapy treats Stacey's physical dependency on alcohol, there may be underlying reasons why Stacey is drinking excessively, such as her feelings of bereavement from the death of her mother, and the use of alcohol for relaxation and to join in social situations. Aversion therapy would not help Stacey manage these underlying issues. She is more likely to relapse if she uses a treatment that only addresses her physical addiction, not her psychological issues.

Ley's cognitive model (1988) would suggest that if Stacey failed to complete the treatment programme it could be due to other factors such a lack of understanding of the long-term effects alcohol may have on her body. Volpp et al. (2009) would suggest that a financial incentive might encourage Stacey to adhere to her treatment programme.

In conclusion, aversion therapy might help Stacey overcome her physical addition to alcohol and change her behaviour, but there are disadvantages such as the risk of side effects, the possibility that she will not continue treatment, and the potential for relapse if underlying psychological problems are not addressed.

Cognitive behavioural therapy may be more beneficial for Stacey, however, as this would teach her to recognise the situations in which she is most likely to drink alcohol and give her strategies to avoid drinking.

Make sure your points are relevant and clearly link to the scenario throughout. Remember that only using a name from the scenario in your answer does not count as a link.

In your conclusion, make sure your points are supported. Here, the points made in the conclusion are linked back to long-term behavioural change and offer a judgement on the possible effectiveness of the treatment.

Now try this

Outline what you would include in response to the following question, which relates to the behavioural scenario on page 106.

Many theories have been used to address addictive behaviour such as Anita's shopping addiction. Evaluate the self-efficacy theory (Bandura, 1977) as a way to explain how Anita could change her addictive shopping behaviour.

Give examples from the behavioural scenario to support your understanding and evaluation of the theory. You could consider alternative views in your answer to help you to reach a conclusion. Refer back to the question in your conclusion to make the links clear.

To revise Bandura's self-efficacy theory, see page 69.

Discuss questions

If you are asked a **discuss** question, you need to consider in detail the different aspects of an issue, situation, problem or argument and how they interrelate.

Qualities when answering a discuss question

Consider how your response to a **discuss** question will:

☑ show accurate and detailed knowledge and understanding

☑ make points that are relevant to the context in the question, showing clear links

☑ display a well-developed and logical discussion that clearly considers a range of different aspects and considers how they interrelate, in a sustained way.

Worked example

Research by psychologists has found that role conflict, the effect of the environment and the level of control can contribute towards stress experienced in the workplace.

Discuss the role of the workplace in explaining Malik's stress.

You must refer to studies in your answer.

This question and sample response extract relates to the stress scenario on page 108. It requires an extended answer, with clear links to the question and the scenario.

Sample response extract

Role conflict in the workplace could be a contributory factor to Malik's stress because he is expected to perform two roles that are incompatible. His role includes protecting employee safety but he is obliged to implement a change in shift patterns that he feels has associated risk. He tried to raise his concerns with management but feels they failed to listen, adding to his stress.

Discuss the points made in relation to the question and scenario, and how they relate to one another.

Due to the change in shift patterns, Malik is working more hours. The environment in the chemical factory is pressurised as Malik tries to enforce health and safety regulations in conditions of high demand with repetitive tasks, in order to safeguard against exposure to fumes and harmful substances. These environmental factors could lead Malik to feel stressed.

Use key terminology correctly to show your knowledge and understanding.

Malik works on a production line. Typically, this type of work has a low level of control as operatives are unable to choose which tasks to do when. Malik is likely to have increased workload as the factory is experiencing increased demand for its products. These factors are both associated with higher levels of stress. Johansson et al. (1978) found that workers had higher levels of physiological and psychological stress in a workplace where tasks were repetitive, and where there was risk of accident due to inattention and productivity pressure. This might apply to Malik as he works on a production line in a factory where there has been an accident, and there are productivity pressures, resulting in additional stress.

If you are asked to refer to studies, use them to support your knowledge and understanding, linking them to the question and the scenario.

However, it is important to consider other factors that might contribute to how Malik experiences stress in the workplace, such as his personality type and locus of control (Rotter, 1966).

Consider other aspects of Malik's stress. A conclusion is not required for discuss questions.

Now try this

Research by psychologists has found that the health belief model can explain addiction. Discuss the health belief model in relation to Stacey's addiction and the likelihood that she will change her behaviour. You must refer to studies in your answer.

This question relates to the physiological addiction scenario on page 107.

 Links To revise the health belief model, see pages 59–61.

Answers

The answers provided here are examples of possible responses. In some cases, other answers may also be possible.

Unit 1 Psychological approaches and applications

1. Cognitive and social approaches

Individual responses. For example:
The social approach has two key assumptions. It proposes that human behaviour is influenced by the social context – other people in our environment affect how we behave. It also proposes that the culture and society in which we are brought up affects our behaviour, as we conform to social norms in our everyday lives.

2. Learning and biological approaches

Individual responses. For example:
The biological approach suggests that nature is the fundamental influence on behaviour. An individual's genetic make-up determines their brain function and neurochemistry, which make them who they are. Behaviour is a product of evolution – no learning is necessary.
On the other hand, the learning approach downplays the role of biology and suggests that nurture is the primary influence on behaviour. Observation, imitation and learning experiences in the environment (starting at birth) influence our behaviour.

3. Reconstructive memory

Individual responses. For example:
Milo lost detail in his recall because of shortening. He condensed the plot to its key elements. Ben recalls Milo telling him about a ghost in the film, because it was a horror film. His schema for horror films includes ghosts, so he confabulated his account.

4. Priming and cognitive scripts

Individual responses. For example:
Putting eyes on the money box might stop people from stealing the produce, because the eyes could prime the consumer to think that they are being watched. Consumers might associate the eyes with surveillance, so act as if someone is watching them and pay for the produce they take. This is an example of semantic priming.

5. Cognitive bias

Individual responses. For example:
Pete may have a personality with a hostile attribution bias. This means that he interprets the actions of others as being deliberately insulting towards him. In this case, he believes that the other person is hostile to him, and acts on that belief by attacking his victim for 'looking at him funny'.

6. The Bartlett study (1932)

Individual responses. For example:
Bartlett (1932) found that the participants shortened the text of the story on each successive recall. He also found that the participants showed evidence of rationalisation and confabulation.

7. The Harris et al. study (2009)

Individual responses. For example:
Harris, Bargh and Brownell (2009) found that showing children adverts for junk food caused them to eat more snacks. They believe that food adverts prime for eating schema, making food consumption more likely. In the context of rising childhood obesity, it is sensible to limit the priming of automatic eating habits in children.

8. The Loftus and Palmer study (1974)

Individual responses. For example:
The word 'smashed' activated a schema in participants which contains the idea of travelling at a high speed, as when something smashes into something else it must be travelling at a greater number of miles per hour. The words 'contacted' or 'hit' do not activate a schema for speed to the same extent as the word 'smashed' does.

9. Social conformity

1 Informational social influence.
Individual responses. For example:
2 Amita has seen what her colleagues wear to work. She is new to her role, so she uses them as a source of information and wears what they wear to conform to the group.

10. Social categorisation

Individual responses. For example:
Liam categorises Jim by occupation and gender, using his assumptions of a typical male builder. Liam has a stereotype of male builders and this includes that they like beer, so he brought an unsuitable gift based on these existing stereotypes.

11. The Asch study (1951)

Individual responses. For example:
Asch (1951) tested participants by putting them individually into groups of actors who were pretending to be other participants. The real participants were always situated last or second to last in the group. Each group member had to call which line, out of a choice of three, matched the standard line. The actors had to give the same wrong answer in 12 of 18 trials. The researcher recorded the participants' answers in these critical trials as either conforming to the group or not.

12. The Chatard et al. study (2007)

Individual responses. For example:
Chatard et al. (2007) showed that gender stereotypes influence people's estimation of their own academic capabilities. Female achievement in maths and male performance in arts tend to be underestimated because they don't fit with generally held stereotypes about male and female characteristics. If males and females underestimate their abilities, they are less likely to choose courses and careers that make the most of their talents. This could limit their opportunities for success in life.

13. The Haney et al. study (1973)

Individual responses. For example:
One weakness is that the study is regarded as being unethical because the participants were not protected from psychological harm – the prisoners were severely stressed in the prison as they were humiliated by the guards. However, it could be argued that this increased the validity of the study as the guards and prisoners showed their natural behaviour, and were not constrained by the ethics of the situation.

14. Classical conditioning

Individual responses. For example:
The balloon pop was an unconditioned stimulus (UCS), causing the unconditioned response (UCR) of fear. The clown was originally a neutral stimulus (NS) that did not cause fear, but because Amina associated him with the fearful noise, he became a conditioned stimulus (CS). Amina now experiences fear, the conditioned response (CR), whenever a clown (CS) is present.

15. Operant conditioning

Individual responses. For example:
The psychologist would explain Viktor's gambling as a product of positive reinforcement. Every time he wins, he is rewarded with money, and the behaviour that led to the win is reinforced. This means he is likely to repeat the behaviour in the future.

16. Social learning theory

Individual responses. For example:
Ben is modelling his behaviour on Dan, who is similar to Ben because they are of the same sex. Dan is older and has higher status, so Ben identifies with him and tries to be like him by imitating his behaviour. The consequence for Dan was to be reinforced for being kind to his little sister. Ben watches all this happening and, in order to be like Ben and receive the same reward, he models Dan's behaviour and is kind to Jade too. This is an example of vicarious reinforcement.

17. The Bandura et al. study (1961)

Individual responses. For example:
Bandura et al. (1961) found that children imitated the behaviour of adults. The children observed what the adults were doing and modelled their behaviour when placed in a similar situation. This happened most when the child and adult were of the same sex – when the adult is similar to the child, the child is more likely to model them.

18. The Watson and Rayner study (1920)

Individual responses. For example:
Watson and Rayner (1920) found that Little Albert, who was not initially afraid of a rat, developed a fear through classical conditioning. Watson and Rayner presented the rat (neutral stimulus) along with a frightening noise (unconditioned stimulus). Albert was fearful (unconditioned response) of the noise. Eventually, Albert showed fear (conditioned response) when presented with the rat (conditioned stimulus), in the absence of the noise.

19. The Skinner study (1932)

Individual responses. For example:
Aim: to demonstrate that rats can learn to press a lever through operant conditioning.
Procedure: a rat will be placed in a controlled environment where there is a lever connected to a food-delivery mechanism. The rat will be rewarded with a food pellet for any behaviour that approximates to lever pressing. Eventually, the rat will only be rewarded when it presses the lever. When it reliably and quickly presses the lever, it will have learned the desired action.

20. Biology and behaviour

Individual responses. For example:
The biological approach focuses on the inheritance of physiology (nature) as an explanation for behaviour, whereas the learning approach focuses on behaviour as a consequence of learning through experience of the environment (nurture).
There is an extended version of this question in the skills section of this book.

21. Evolutionary psychology

Individual responses. For example:
Humans still have the fight-or-flight response due to genome lag. Genes that suited us to life in the environment of evolutionary adaptation are still dominant in our genome, because it takes thousands of years for genes to change. The environment today is very different, so those genes that cause the fight-or-flight response are no longer advantageous but still present.

22. The Buss et al. study (1992)

Individual responses. For example:
Kaz is worried about Al falling in love as, according to the findings of Buss et al. (1992), there is an evolutionary pressure on females to maintain romantic relationships in order to secure resources, such as food and protection. According to the findings, if Al was having sex with another woman this would not stop him being in a relationship with her. If he loved someone else, he would not share his resources with Kaz.

23. The Deady et al. study (2006)

Individual responses. For example:
Deady et al. (2006) found a negative correlation between maternal ambition and testosterone level, suggesting that the higher the testosterone level, the less likely the woman is to want to be a mother.

24. The Harlow study (1868)

Individual responses. For example:
Case studies, like Harlow's (1868) study of Gage, are useful in neuropsychology as they help to build a map of the brain by linking loss of function to a site of brain damage. However, they lack reliability as each case is individual and brain damage is hard to assess exactly. It is difficult to establish population validity using single case studies.

25. Cognitive approach to aggression

Individual responses. For example:
Fina experienced domestic violence as a child and so developed her own schema for violence. She has cognitive scripts for aggressive behaviour that can be primed by domestic disagreements.

26. Social approach to aggression

Individual responses. For example:
The anti-social behaviour of the 2011 riots could be explained through both normative and informational social influence. If young people want to be part of a gang that is engaged in anti-social behaviour, they are likely to engage in that behaviour to fit in. This is normative social influence. The opinions of anti-social activists were publicised on social media, so some young people would have had access to them. They may have thought these opinions were correct. If young people come to believe it is acceptable to loot from shops, they might think they are doing something reasonable in the circumstances. This is informational social influence.

27. Learning approach to aggression

Individual responses. For example:
The footballer might not repeat the aggression because he was immediately punished by being sent off. This means that, in future, he might associate aggression with punishment and is less likely to be aggressive to avoid being punished.

28. Biological approach to aggression

Individual responses. For example:
Terry might be programmed by his genes to be aggressive. As his father and brother have similar issues and they all share genes, it is likely that the aggression is inherited. Genes could lead to high levels of testosterone or to differences in brain structure that predispose this family towards aggression that is hard to control.

29. Cognitive approach to business

Individual responses. For example:
When the drink is red, learners are primed to think that it is flavoured with a red fruit, so they are likely to say that it is cherry-flavoured. This is because their schema for red drinks do not include lemonade. When they cannot see the colour, different schema are triggered, such as for flavour.

30. Social approach to business

1 Informational social influence.
Individual responses. For example:
2 Social proof is involved as worm graphs enable viewers to watch the reaction of other voters. Viewers may assume that

other voters are acting on superior information, and they might base their opinion about the debate simply on what others seem to be thinking.

31. Learning approach to business

Individual responses. For example:
Eden Hazard is a top football player and Nike produce football kit. Hazard is a role model for people who like football and if he is observed using Nike kit, those people who identify with Hazard might also want to use the kit. This means they could be more likely to buy Nike's products.

32. Biological approach to business

Individual responses. For example:
Biological concepts such as localisation of function and research techniques such as brain scanning can be used to influence consumer behaviour. By understanding how the brain responds to stimuli in the environment, it is possible to manipulate the environment to cause a specific response in the consumer. Neuromarketing uses techniques such as eye-tracking in order to detect and measure the direction and duration of gaze at aspects of an advert or a product. In this way, adverts can be manipulated so our attention is drawn to them and their message. Research in this area shows that adults focus their attention on images of babies and especially on what babies are looking at. So an effective advert may show the baby looking at the message that the advertisers want to convey.
Techniques like these are more reliable and accurate than asking people for their opinion of the product, because people don't always give truthful responses. They may want to manage how they appear to others, or be uncertain about how they feel. This means that the techniques used in neuromarketing are efficient, and only the most effective adverts make it to public campaigns.

33. Cognitive approach to gender

Individual responses. For example:
Gender dysphoria is a condition in which the person is biologically one sex but psychologically feels that this is wrong for them.

34. Social approach to gender

Individual responses. For example:
There are gender stereotypes for the kinds of behaviours which males and females are expected to exhibit. Stephen uses a stereotype that boys are more physical than girls and dismisses the behaviour as being normal for boys. By playing in a very physical way, boys are conforming to gender norms.

35. Learning approach to gender

Individual responses. For example:
Tia is being positively reinforced by her mum's laughter for the lipstick use. This means she is likely to repeat the behaviour in the future and learns through operant conditioning.
Joe is less likely to use behaviour that is modelled by a female. He will pay more attention to males in his environment and they are unlikely to use lipstick, so he will not learn to use it either.

36. Biological approach to gender

Individual responses. For example:
Andi might have experienced atypical prenatal development. The male hormone testosterone might not have had the usual effect on Andi's developing brain, which was not masculinised. This could explain why Andi experiences gender dysphoria.

37. Your Unit 1 exam

Your notes on the Unit 1 exam, always referring to the latest Sample Assessment Material on the Pearson website for an indication of assessment details.

38. Understanding scenarios

Individual responses. For example:
Lewis Hamilton is a good choice as he could be a role model for children, maybe boys in particular, who are interested in cars. As he is a world champion racing driver, he has high status, so children are likely to identify with him. They might want to imitate any of Lewis's behaviour they are capable of, in order to get similar rewards to him. So the manufacturers expect that children will want to have the car if they see Lewis playing with the toy, increasing sales as children ask for it for Christmas.

39. Identify and give questions

Individual responses. For example:
1   Star charts are a form of operant conditioning because they aim to change behaviour by controlling its consequences.
2   Positive reinforcement happens when the child is given a reward such as a star or a treat for their behaviour.

40. State and name questions

Informational social influence **or** normative social influence.

41. Describe questions

Individual responses. For example:
Priming can be used to change people's buying behaviour. It can be used to influence how we think about products and make us more likely to buy something. Priming activates a schema that affects how we behave. A prime such as green packaging can automatically make us think that the product is environmentally friendly, which might change our opinion of the product and influence our buying decision.

42. Justify and interpret questions

Individual responses. For example:
Operant conditioning states that we learn from the consequences of our actions. If we do something and receive a reward, we experience positive reinforcement. If our action leads to avoidance of a punishment then we experience negative reinforcement. In both cases this increases the probability of the act occurring again. If the act is punished, the probability of it occurring again is reduced.

43. Explain questions (short)

Individual responses. For example:
Bandura et al. (1961) showed that children's behaviour changed according to the actions of the models they had watched. Children who were shown a model that behaved aggressively were later aggressive themselves, unlike those who did not see the model behave aggressively. This shows how behaviour is learned through the observation and imitation of what other people do.

44–45. Analyse questions

Individual responses. Here is an example of outline notes for one answer:
- Outline key ideas in social learning that can be used to analyse the development of gender: indirect experience, learning through observation of models that the person identifies with, models having similarity to the actor, link to gender, boys imitate males more than they do females.
- Analyse the process by which children learn gender behaviour: for example, children pay attention to same-sex parents and are likely to be reinforced for imitating gendered behaviour, such as little girls playing with dolls.
- Analyse how the media can affect modelling, for example, same-sex characters on TV programmes being reinforced for gender-consistent behaviour. It is impossible to say how much of an influence this is because it is so embedded in family and cultural life.
- Select the most appropriate psychological research/theory/ concept to support. For example, Bandura et al.'s (1961) research showed children were more likely to imitate same-sex

models, adding support to the analysis of the role of social learning.

46–47. Assess questions

Individual responses for a brief answer plan. For example:
- Outline the biological approach and link to aggression: warrior gene, testosterone, brain structure.
- Outline the link between evolution and male aggression.
- Evidence – Phineas Gage study – explain how biological changes led to change in aggression.
- Difficult to test role of biology – genes run in families but so does environment.
- Social learning might be better – Bandura et al. (1961) showed direct link.

48–49. Compare questions

Individual responses for the answer plan. For example:
- Biological approach takes nature view (innate, genes, brain chemistry/structure).
- Learning approach is nurture (learning from direct or indirect experience in the environment).
- Biological approach argues for evolutionary pressures for males being more aggressive – hunting/protection; adaptive advantage.
- Learning approach argues that it depends on cultural reinforcements – males have more aggressive models.
- Both approaches explain aggressive behaviour as something that is not directly controlled by the individual but as a product of either nature or nurture.

50–51. Discuss questions

Individual responses to the answer plan. For example:
- Learning approach key assumption – behaviour learned through exposure to environment.
- Social learning theory: explain – link to advertising – celebrity advertising.
- Widely used so must be effective – evidence for social learning theory – Bandura et al. (1961).
- Operant conditioning – use of loyalty cards to positively reinforce shopping at certain shop.
- Backed up by research showing how behaviour changes as a result of rewards (Skinner, 1932)

52–53. Explain questions (long)

Individual responses for the answer plan. For example:
- Cognitive approach explains behaviour as a result of information processing.
- Outline hostile attribution bias.
- Link to aggression – give an example to illustrate.
- Outline priming.
- Link to activation of aggressive schema – give an example to illustrate.

54. Evaluate questions

Individual responses that may include the following, for example:
- Bandura et al.'s (1961) study was conducted in a laboratory setting, which makes it very reliable.
- All the variables that might have affected the children's behaviour were controlled.
- For example, he made sure they all had the same toys to play with at the end, so you can be sure that the only thing that differed was the behaviour of the adult. You can conclude that this is what made them more or less aggressive.
- On the other hand, it could be argued that the use of the laboratory setting made the study low in ecological validity, as the children were subjected to unusual experiences that they might not encounter in their everyday lives.
- For example, the children were left alone in a strange room to play with toys, so it may be that they only learn from models in such controlled conditions.

- In conclusion, the study has both strengths and weaknesses, but it was a well-controlled experiment which clearly showed the effect of modelling on behaviour.

Unit 3 Health psychology

55. Health and ill heath

Individual responses. For example:
- The biomedical model focuses on the biological aspects of health and ill health and the medical identification and treatment of physical symptoms. It suggests a person is healthy if they have the absence of disease.
- The biopsychosocial model is a holistic approach that includes the medical/biological aspects of the biomedical model along with factors that relate to psychological and social well-being.
- Health as a continuum places the biological, psychological and social aspects of health on a continuum. Health is a position on the continuum determined by the combination of these factors, not an either/or state of either health or ill health.

56. Behavioural and physiological addiction

Individual responses. For example:
- **Behavioural addiction** is when a person repeatedly and compulsively engages in a particular behaviour, even if the behaviour causes them harm. Behavioural addictions include gambling and shopping.
- **Physiological addiction** is when physical symptoms result from use of or withdrawal from the substance, such as in addiction to cocaine or nicotine.

57. Griffiths' components of addiction

Individual responses. For example:
1. The alcoholic may demonstrate **dependence** on alcohol as this becomes the most important thing in their life.
2. **Tolerance** could be exhibited, so they have to drink more alcohol to have the same feelings.
3. If they do not drink alcohol, they could experience physiological or psychological **withdrawal**.
4. If the alcoholic gives up drinking alcohol but decides to have just one drink, they could **relapse** into their previous drinking behaviours.
5. The addict may experience **conflict** with family members. They may also feel intrapsychic conflict if they know they shouldn't drink but feel they can't stop.
6. The addict may enjoy the **mood changes** that alcohol creates.

58. Stress

Individual responses. For example:
Stress is a physiological and/or a psychological response to the environment or situation. It occurs when an individual is presented with a demanding set of circumstances that exceed their perceived ability to cope.

59. Rosenstock's health belief model

Perceived seriousness: 'My grandfather had a stroke but recovered completely.'
Perceived susceptibility: 'My chances of getting liver cancer are actually very low.'

60. The Becker study (1978)

Individual responses. For example:
According to the HBM, perceived benefits (and costs) influence people's health decisions. The cost to Jay and Max of the asthma attack was cancellation of their holiday, which may have lost them money and impacted on their special family time. Becker et al. (1978) found that people who are aware of the costs of an asthma attack, in terms of interruption of their arrangements, are more likely to be compliant.

61. The Carpenter study (2010)

Individual responses. For example:
According to Carpenter (2010), perceived barriers are more important influences on behaviour than any other aspect of the HBM. Therefore, removal of barriers should help people with depression adhere to advice in the health promotion campaign. Ways to remove barriers could include making sure that the repeat prescription service is fast and easy to use, counselling sessions take place at a convenient place and time, and that information on exercise and healthy eating is available through the website.

62. Rotter's locus of control

Individual responses. For example:
Tom believes that his smoking relapse has been caused by his boyfriend's behaviour, an external factor. This shows that Tom thinks he has no control over his own smoking habits. Therefore, he has an external locus of control.

63. The Rotter study (1966)

Individual responses. For example:
Since Erin has an internal locus of control and feels able to influence outcomes in her life, she is more likely to be successful in making health-related behaviour change, such as giving up smoking. Rotter (1966) found that people with an internal locus, although less likely to smoke in the first place, are more able to give up when they decide to make the change, due to their sense of self-belief.

64. The Abouserie study (1994)

Individual responses. For example:
The scenario suggests that Gabe, who feels he can't influence his exam grades by working hard, has an external locus of control, which Abouserie (1994) found is associated with higher levels of academic stress. Counselling could help Gabe develop more control over his studies and take responsibility for his exam outcomes, moving him towards an internal locus of control. This should reduce Gabe's stress levels as, according to Abouserie (1994), people with an internal locus of control feel less academic stress.

65. The Krause study (1986)

Individual responses. For example:
The scenario suggests that Marjory probably has an extreme internal locus of control – she has been organised and in control when moving home in the past but is feeling very stressed now she can't manage the situation herself. As someone with an extreme internal locus of control, Marjory is likely to use coping mechanisms to deal with stress. Removing herself from the source of stress by visiting her sister during the move is a coping mechanism.

66. Ajzen's theory of planned behaviour

Individual responses. For example:
Personal attitude – Alex has positive feelings towards gambling as he feels he often wins.
Subjective norms – Alex's family want him to stop gambling.
Perceived behavioural control – As Alex finds gambling online easy to do and feels he often wins, he may find it difficult to carry out behavioural change.

67. The Louis et al. study (2009)

Individual responses. For example:
Perceived control is an aspect of the TPB that relates to how easy a person feels it will be to carry out a planned behaviour, for example to eat healthily. Barriers are things that people think will make it hard for them to act. According to Louis et al. (2009), perceived control and barriers are important in whether people plan to eat healthily or unhealthily. Since students have commented that price is a barrier to healthy eating, this is something that Clive should address.

68. The Cooke et al. study (2016)

Individual responses. For example:
1   Matias boasts about how much alcohol he can drink, which implies he is confident (has high self-efficacy) in his ability to consume it.
2   According to Cooke et al. (2016), people with high self-efficacy tend to drink more.

69. Bandura's self-efficacy theory

Individual responses. For example:
1   Outcome expectancy – Sarah is aware of the health effects of smoking, which may contribute to her desire to give up. She also knows she will feel relaxed when she smokes, so she may be tempted to continue smoking.
2   Mastery experiences – Sarah has failed to give up smoking in the past, so she may lack the self-belief to help her succeed in the future.
3   Vicarious reinforcement – Sarah's parents were role models for smoking, making it more likely that she starts in the first place.
4   Social persuasion – Sarah's friends say she should give up, which may influence her behaviour.
5   Emotional state – Sarah is anxious, which could make giving up hard for her.

70. The Bandura and Adams study (1977)

Individual responses. For example:
1   Through treatment, Rafal has improved outcome expectancy as he now thinks he may be able look at a spider, whereas previously he believed his phobia could not be changed. According to the self-efficacy theory, better outcome expectancy is associated with improved self-efficacy.
2   According to Bandura and Adams (1977), high self-efficacy is associated with behaviour change. Rafal's treatment for spider phobia is more likely to be successful if he feels greater self-efficacy. If Rafal can control his spider phobia, he will no longer experience severe anxiety, sweating and nausea when he sees a spider.

71. The Marlatt et al. study (1995)

1   Kayden would most benefit from support to stop smoking.
Individual responses. For example:
2   Kayden has low coping self-efficacy, so is least likely to be able to change his behaviour. Marlatt et al. (1995) recommended using levels of self-efficacy to target support to those most at risk from difficulty with addiction and using treatments that raise self-efficacy. With improved self-efficacy, Kayden is more likely to be successful in quitting.

72. Life events and daily hassles

Individual responses. For example:
Research has found that some scales are better for measuring stress than others. For example, Kanner et al. (1981) found that daily hassles measured with the HUS, such as Frank's car not starting and his computer crashing, are better predictors of stress than life events measured with the SRRS. This suggests that Frank is likely to feel more stressed than Ranj and that the HUS is more useful than the SRRS. However, people cope differently with stress, so their individual situations may not support the findings.

73. Workplace stress

Individual responses. For example:
Sion could be given greater **level of control** over the order in which he completes tasks, so that the work is less monotonous. Sion's manager could consult with him on his **workload** to set more realistic deadlines. Sion might prefer to share an office, so that there are other people in the **environment**.

74. Personality and stress

Individual responses. For example:
- Hardy personalities will see the approaching game as a challenge rather than a threat. They are more likely to prepare for the match by training hard and finding out about the other team's strengths.
- Type A personalities will be impatient to get on with the match, and are likely to feel competitive and aggressive.
- Type B players will be relaxed about the match and may feel that reaching the final is a great achievement, irrespective of the score on the day.

75. General adaptation syndrome

Individual responses. For example:
If Steve's body remains on high alert, it will deal with the long-term stress by continuing to secrete cortisol. Eventually, his resources will be used up and his body will enter the third stage of the GAS, exhaustion. He won't be able to fight the stressor, will feel very tired and his immune system may become weakened, leaving him susceptible to illness.

76. Sympathomedullary pathway

Individual responses. For example:
Acute stress is short term and occurs in one-off situations. For example, getting into trouble at college might cause acute stress.

77. Hypothalamic-pituitary-adrenal system

Individual responses. For example:
Daisy may have:
- psychological effects – these could include sleep and memory problems, depression and anxiety.
- physical effects – high blood pressure, headaches, digestive issues and weight gain, muscle weakness and poor immune function.

78. Role of adrenaline

Individual responses. For example:
Oliver may be prescribed beta blockers to help him deal with the short-term stress of his examinations. Stress is causing his body to release adrenaline – this makes his heart race and causes him to sweat.
The medication blocks the effects of the increased adrenaline within his body, preventing the signs and symptoms of stress.

79. Physiological gender differences

Individual responses. For example:
Gender can impact on how stress is exhibited. Diane is losing sleep and comfort-eating, while Matt is showing aggressive behaviour. Diane and Matt may be experiencing the physiological response to stress of the release of four key hormones of adrenaline, testosterone, cortisol and oxytocin. Matt's aggression may reflect higher levels of testosterone, and Diane's less aggressive response may reflect higher levels of oxytocin. However, it would be limiting to view their response in purely physiological terms as this may be too simplistic. Their behaviour may reflect traditional role expectations and may also be learned. Other males in the same position may not react aggressively to such stresses and other females may not lose sleep or comfort eat. Individuals respond to stress differently for many reasons and the physiological response relating to gender is one consideration among many.

80. Freeze response

Individual responses. For example:
Dave, Sajii and Stu all experience the same physiological reactions to acute stress caused by the car crash, but all have different responses. Dave demonstrates the flight response by running away, Sajii feels aggressive and shows a fight response, while Stu is frozen to the spot because his cognitive functions are temporarily impaired. The reactions of the three people show that other factors influence responses to events, not just physiological changes.

81. Fight-or-flight response

Individual responses. For example:
The fight-or-flight response is an evolutionary adaptation to stresses from prehistoric times. The changes that this response causes in Freda's body do not help her deal with the long-term stress of moving home and starting a new job. The physiological changes in her body are experienced psychologically as anxiety. If her stress remains heightened, there are additional health risks. This maladaptive response illustrates that there are evolutionary reasons for stress, not just physiological ones, and these can have wide-ranging effects.

82. Role of personality

Individual responses. For example:
Li Wei's response to the stress of doing the presentation is likely to be different from Claire's, due to their personality types. Li Wei, Type A, may show visible signs of stress by frowning at the audience due to his tense facial muscles. He may be flustered if he is asked questions. Claire, due to her Type B personality, is likely to respond in a less stressed manner.
This suggests that their personality type as well as their physiological response will influence their behaviour when under the stress of delivering a presentation.

83. Stress and ill health

Individual responses. For example:
Kiecolt-Glaser et al. (1984) found there were more white blood cells present in student blood samples a month before their examinations and fewer white blood cells at exam time, due to stress. A decrease in the number of her white blood cells at exam time could mean that Jenny is more susceptible to a cold than normal.
Exams cause stress and therefore an increase in the body's cortisol levels. This brings about the immunosuppression that Jenny is experiencing.

84. Stress and the cardiac system

Individual responses. For example:
Priya has chronic stress so has been exposed to high levels of cortisol and adrenaline, which is likely to have a negative effect on her cardiac health. Her working situation and stress cause her to make unhealthy lifestyle choices, such as poor diet and lack of exercise, which are also bad for her cardiac health.
These factors can all lead to high blood pressure and long-term cardiac ill health.

85. Biological approach to smoking

Individual responses. For example:
As Olivia and Helena are identical twins, they share genetic factors. Vink et al. (2005) found that although smoking behaviour has a large genetic component, other factors such as the environment and social situation also have an effect.
As the twins are identical, if Olivia has the DRD2 gene then Helena would also have the same gene, and so could be predisposed to become addicted to smoking if she tried it. Social and environmental factors, such as friendship groups and opportunities to smoke, could determine whether she does actually start smoking.
Olivia and Helena's situation supports the argument that factors in addition to genetics influence smoking addiction.

86. Learning approach to smoking

Individual responses. For example:
Social learning theory suggests that we pay attention to role models around us. Dannie may view his family members, especially his older brother, as his role models. Dannie may experience vicarious reinforcement of smoking if he sees his family members enjoying positive feelings of relaxation while smoking. He may try smoking in order to experience the same consequences.

Dannie's whole family smokes. He may feel more accepted if he also smokes. This provides positive reinforcement for the behaviour.

87. Cognitive approach to alcohol

Individual responses. For example:
Kara is self-medicating with alcohol to cope with the stress of entertaining clients and negotiating deals. Alcohol helps Kara relax so she feels more confident – she believes alcohol makes her more effective at her job, so she maintains the habit.
Kara is finding that she needs to drink increasing amounts of alcohol to achieve the same feelings of relaxation and confidence, so she is developing a dependency on alcohol.

88. Learning approach to alcohol

Individual responses. For example:
Trevon's drinking behaviour is being influenced by his new peer group. If Trevon admires role models who drink heavily, he is more likely to drink too.
He has a fantastic time when he is out drinking and dancing, so he experiences positive reinforcement for his behaviour and is likely to repeat it.
When Trevon is hungover, he is experiencing the negative effects of alcohol. When he has another drink, the symptoms of hangover improve and Trevon's drinking is negatively reinforced. This means he is more likely to repeat the behaviour.

89. Cognitive approach to gambling

Individual responses. For example:
The cognitive approach explains long-term maintenance of Doug's gambling through the concepts of irrational thoughts and cognitive bias.
Doug may think, irrationally, that if he wills the fruit images to line up, they will do so and he will win. This is irrational because the fruit machine mechanism is not within his control – he has an illusion of control.
Doug also has cognitive bias because he has a ritualistic behaviour (playing the machines in the same order) which he believes helps him to win.

90. Learning approach to gambling

Individual responses. For example:
Variable ratio reinforcement, as used by fruit machines, creates a steady rate of response but offers a reward after an unpredictable number of responses. Aki may feel that the machine he is playing will pay out if he plays for long enough.

91. Learning approach to shopping

Individual responses. For example:
Learning theories suggest that Kev's shopping may become more extreme in this situation.
Kev is already addicted to shopping, so experiences positive reinforcement for his behaviour. This might come from the buzz that he experiences when he purchases new sportswear. Kev's favourite basketball player is a role model and Kev aspires to be like him. Kev's shopping addiction may become worse if he feels compelled to purchase sports gear that is promoted by his role model. If the role model appears to be positively reinforced by using the products, perhaps with enhanced sporting performance, Kev may experience vicarious reinforcement by using the same products.

92. Cognitive approach to shopping

Individual responses. For example:
Several aspects of the scenario suggest that Holly has an addiction. Holly has had depression and may be using shopping to self-medicate. She will probably feel excitement when she makes a purchase, which will distract her from the feelings she has about the relationship breakdown. Holly may be feeling anxious about the debt she is accumulating. Continuing to shop may relieve these negative feelings. Holly has a cognitive bias regarding her level of control as she thinks she can give up shopping but hasn't actually done so.

93. Hovland–Yale theory of persuasion

Here are four possible options for Franca.
1   As **communicator** of the new programme, Franca needs to influence learners (**message recipients**) at the college. She can do this by developing her expertise in the environmental problems associated with plastics and the solutions, and by being personable and approachable when people want to find out more. She needs the support of key figures, such as the principal and popular teachers.
2   Franca's **communication** could be emotive, for example using images of distressed wildlife caught up in plastic waste, and could use fear messages, such as statistics on the number of plastic bottles disposed of annually.
3   Franca needs to think about the **characteristics of the message recipients**. Some learners will be motivated by rewards and others by how easy it is to make the transition to a new behaviour. The college council could set targets for reducing use of plastic bottles and supply reusable bottles free of charge. The availability of water fountains may be important, so that learners don't have to queue for refills.
4   Franca can make her campaign **credible** by using supporting information from expert organisations such as Greenpeace and Friends of the Earth. She could align her programme with national campaigns such as Greenpeace's 'Take the plastics pledge' or Friends of the Earth's 'My World My Home' initiative for young people.

94. Hovland–Yale application

Here are four possible aspects of applying the Hovland–Yale theory:
1   The **communicator** is a trusted expert. According to the Hovland–Yale model and Hovland and Weiss (1951), this increases the effectiveness of communication.
2   Parents are the **recipients** of the message. Many personal factors, such as gender, IQ and cultural background influence whether they will be persuaded by the message to have their children vaccinated. The need for cognition is high because the complex message is difficult to understand. This could decrease the effectiveness of the communication.
3   **Communication** takes the form of a fear appeal, which can be initially effective. However, the message may be less effective over time. The message has an emotional component, making it more persuasive, since it is about the recipients' children.
4   As a respected doctor, the source is highly **credible**.
The Hovland–Yale (1951) theory suggests that this campaign could be successful in persuading parents to change their behaviour and have their children vaccinated. The persuasiveness of the campaign could be increased by making the message easier to understand, decreasing the need for cognition by the recipients.

95. The fear arousal theory

Individual responses. For example:
Fear arousal is used to gain the attention of the audience and to help them understand the message so they change their behaviour. In the case of using picture warnings on cigarette packets, the target audience was current smokers. Showing frightening images of damage caused by smoking, pitched at medium fear arousal, increases the likelihood of people understanding and remembering the consequences of smoking, and then carrying out the desired behaviour of quitting. The level of fear arousal must be pitched above low (which leads to boredom with the message) and below high (which leads to denial and suppression of the message).

96. Elaboration-likelihood model

Neelam used the central (high) route to persuasion.

97. Stress management 1

Individual responses. For example:
Jo could benefit from a form of relaxation training to help her through the temporary stressful situation of learning to drive and taking her test. Jo could try using visualisations in which she sees herself driving confidently and passing her test. Meditation and yoga would also help train her body to relax in stressful situations.

98. Stress management 2

Individual responses. For example:
Kirra could use drug treatment (physiological method) and stress inoculation treatment (psychological treatment) to cope with work stress.
A similarity is that both drug treatment and stress inoculation treatment would enable Kirra to cope with the daily experience of her work stress.
Differences between the approaches:
- Drug treatment, such as beta blockers if suitable, would control Kirra's symptoms of stress in the short term but would not remove the stressor itself.
- Stress inoculation treatment would equip Kirra with the skills to cope with the stressors as they reoccur, offering a potentially long-term solution.

99. Addiction treatments 1

Individual responses. For example:
There are benefits of aversion therapy with disulfiram. Aversion therapy could help Shane stop drinking by breaking the pleasurable associations which drinking has for him. Instead, drinking alcohol would become associated with being sick. If Shane was able to give up drinking alcohol, his overall health and well-being would improve and his risk of certain diseases, such as cancer and liver disease, would decrease.
There are disadvantages of this type of therapy. If Shane realises the aversion therapy medication is making him ill, he may just stop taking it and relapse. There may be side effects of taking the drug. This treatment doesn't address the underlying problems that may have caused Shane's alcoholism in the first place. This treatment doesn't help alleviate withdrawal symptoms, but could be combined with other therapies to address this.

100. Addiction treatments 2

Individual responses. For example:
Billie might undergo a drug therapy for his drug addiction. This would help to alleviate any physiological withdrawal symptoms and anxiety he might experience when he stops taking the addictive drug. However, Billie should be aware of the possibility of becoming addicted to the therapeutic drug as well as or instead of the addictive drug. This is particularly important if Billie doesn't address the underlying reasons for his drug addiction.
Billie could combine drug therapy with a psychological therapy, such as cognitive behavioural therapy. In CBT Billie would work with a therapist to address the dysfunctional thinking that has led to his addiction. He would learn to replace his negative thoughts and emotions with positive thinking for the future. CBT takes time and requires personal motivation for change, but it offers a long-term solution to the underlying issues that led to Billie's addiction.

101. Rational non-adherence

Individual responses that might include the following points, for example:
Four factors influence adherence and non-adherence:
1 Cost–benefit analysis – participants analyse the costs and benefits of taking part in the programme, versus the costs and benefits of relapse into an unhealthy lifestyle and weight gain. The programme should promote the benefits of weight loss (and mention the costs of being overweight) to improve adherence.
2 Financial barriers – to improve adherence, the cost of taking part in the programme should not be a barrier. Costs could include membership of the programme, the cost of exercising and the cost of heathy eating. The programme could suggest ways to decrease costs, such as by offering a discount for long-term programme membership, suggesting free ways to exercise such as walking, and providing low-cost healthy menu suggestions.
3 Lack of understanding – the programme should avoid jargon, giving participants clear goals and easy-to-follow instructions on how these can be achieved.
4 Patient–practitioner relationship – participants are more likely to adhere to the weight-loss programme if they have a good relationship with the programme leader and trust them to support their weight-loss journey.

102. Ley's cognitive model

Individual responses that might include the following points, for example:
1 Jagdeep's patients may not understand the terminology used to describe their conditions, or the benefits of taking their medication.
2 They may not remember the information that the GP told them in the consultation. They may also find it hard to recall the directions for taking the medication.
3 Jagdeep's patients may be unsatisfied with the medical advice they received, especially if they felt the GP didn't take the time to explain their illness and treatment in a way that was easy to understand.

103. Adherence and physiology

Individual responses. For example:
Lustman et al. (2000) found that people with diabetes and depression actually manage their condition much better – measured through the use of blood tests – when taking an antidepressant medication compared to a placebo.
If Moses is prescribed an antidepressant for his depression, Lustman et al.'s findings suggest that he may improve his adherence to his diabetes treatment and improve his overall health outcomes.

104. Adherence and psychology

Individual responses. For example:
Volpp et al. (2009) found that adherence to a smoking cessation programme could be increased if participants were paid a financial incentive. Assuming that Volpp et al.'s findings in relation to nicotine addiction can be linked to other substance addictions, Imran could use financial or other reward incentives to improve adherence to a drug treatment programme. A financial incentive or other reward is a positive reinforcement of desired behaviour change.

105. Your Unit 3 exam

Your notes on the Unit 3 exam, always referring to the latest Sample Assessment Material on the Pearson website for an indication of assessment details.

106. Understanding scenarios 1

Individual responses. For example:
1 Anita is keeping her online shopping a secret from her friends.
2 Anita knows her shopping has negative financial consequences, but won't admit there is a problem and falsely believes she can control her behaviour.

107. Understanding scenarios 2

Individual responses. For example:

Aversion therapies use the principles of conditioning (learning approach) to treat substance addictions. Pairing a drug such as disulfiram with alcohol causes vomiting. So if Stacey takes disulfiram and then drinks alcohol, it will make her vomit. In this way, alcohol becomes dissociated from feelings of emotional relief or relaxation for Stacey, and instead is associated with the negative consequence of vomiting. Stacey is less likely to drink alcohol if she has been conditioned to be sick every time she takes a drink.

108. Understanding scenarios 3

Individual responses. For example:

Life changes could have negative effects for Malik's health. For example, life changes for Malik include moving house, the death of a close friend and the accident at work. According to Rahe et al. (1970) life changes such as his daughter's wedding can correlate with ill health, so Malik might become ill.
Daily hassles such as Malik losing his keys and his computer crashing cause stress. According to Kanner et al. (1981) daily hassles correlate with psychological stress, so Malik might experience psychological ill health.

109. Identify and define questions

Individual responses. For example:

CBT is a psychological treatment that can be used to manage Anita's addictive behaviour. Anita could use CBT to help her identify and adapt her thoughts and feelings. Over a period of time working with a therapist to identify and challenge her thinking, the theory is that Anita would replace the dysfunctional beliefs with positive ones to alleviate her shopping addiction.

110. Describe questions

Individual responses. For example:

The first stage of stress inoculation treatment is cognitive preparation. Malik could identify his stressors such as life changes (downsizing), daily hassles (losing keys) and work stress (longer hours and the workplace accident). His practitioner could use the interview to establish which physiological effects of stress are affecting Malik.
The second stage is skill acquisition. Malik could learn visualisation or coping routines to manage stressful situations. The third stage is application and follow-through. When Malik feels stress at home or work, he must use the skills he has learned to deal with the stressors.

111. Explain questions

Individual responses. For example:

A Type A personality is more susceptible to stress than a Type B or hardy personality type. This means that Malik is likely to be susceptible to stress as he multitasks in response to life changes (downsizing), daily hassles (computer crashing) and work stressors (accident investigation) that are taking place. Malik's responses to stressors in his life include irritability, sleeplessness and shutting himself away from his family. As Malik is susceptible to stress, he is experiencing physiological effects and may be developing health conditions that could be associated with chronic stress, such as high blood pressure and coronary heart disease.

112–13. Assess questions

Individual responses may include some of the following points, for example:
- Malik's doctor could give him beta blockers (acebutolol) to reduce activity of adrenaline and noradrenaline in his sympathomedullary pathway, and help him manage his physiological symptoms. Adrenaline and noradrenaline are produced in response to the stressors he is experiencing.
- Medication could reduce the physical symptoms of Malik's stress, such as increased heart rate and dizziness.
- Malik's doctor may prescribe beta blockers for a short period of time as these could be effective in helping Malik deal with the stressful event of his friend dying and the accident at work. Then, when his response stabilises, Malik can reduce the medication.
- Beta blockers will only relieve Malik's symptoms of stress rather than tackling the cause. This means they are ineffective as a long-term stress management strategy.
- However, beta blockers could help Malik deal with immediate stressful life events and support him to start a long-term psychological treatment such as stress inoculation treatment.
- Stress inoculation treatment is a cognitive behavioural therapy where the therapist will ask Malik to go through three distinct stages. In stage 1, cognitive preparation, he will need to be aware of the thoughts he has when in a stressful situation, such as managing the sale of his friend's house.
- In stage 2, skill acquisition, Malik will need to learn effective coping strategies and relaxation techniques. For example, by imagining himself in a situation that causes him stress and carrying out deep breathing exercises.
- In stage 3, application and follow-through, Malik has to ensure that he uses the skills the therapist has taught him if faced with a stressful situation. This will help Malik to manage his stress at home and work.
- To be effective, SIT requires investment from the individual in terms of time and money. Malik may not see changes in his behaviour for a number of weeks or months when using the therapy.
- SIT addresses the cause of the problem and is effective in teaching long-term transferable coping strategies.
- Beta blockers can be effective in treating acute stress in the short term but do not offer Malik a long-term solution to his problems. SIT is an effective treatment that addresses the cause of the stress, in order to make long-lasting changes and improvements to Malik's life experience. The treatments could be more effective as a treatment for Malik's behaviour if used in combination with each other, as this could reduce the impact of the biological and psychological implications of stress on Malik.

114–15. Evaluate questions

Individual responses may include the following points, for example:
- Bandura (1977) developed the self-efficacy theory to describe the factors that influence a person's ability to make behaviour change and move away from addiction. It is possible to apply Bandura's analysis to Anita's situation, to assess which factors might support her if she decides to stop her shopping addiction and which factors would prevent her making this behavioural change.
- Self-efficacy theory states that self-belief influences a person's ability to accomplish a task and produce a favourable outcome. If Anita has high self-efficacy, she is more likely to be able to stop shopping as she believes in her ability to give it up. If she has low self-efficacy, she is likely to lack the self-belief to make change and may continue to shop.
- As a successful business owner with favourable online presence, Anita might have high self-efficacy. However, Anita's additional experience of social anxiety, depression and low self-esteem could influence her self-efficacy, reducing her ability to change behaviour.
- Bandura (1977) identified five factors that influence a person's self-efficacy, such as Anita's. These are outcome expectancy, mastery experiences, vicarious reinforcement, social persuasion and emotional state.
- Outcome expectancy: Anita knows that shopping makes her feel good and that winning an online auction gives her a buzz. Anita's outcome expectancy could make it difficult for her to give up shopping.

- Anita has experienced mastery as she has built up a successful business. Her business of interior design requires planned shopping to a budget, so Anita knows how to shop in a controlled and effective manner for her clients. Anita's mastery could increase her self-efficacy and help her change her behaviour.
- Vicarious reinforcement: Anita has role models in her industry whom she aspires to imitate. She observes them shopping for their work in high-end furniture stores. If she sees them being reinforced by their clients for making excellent purchases, Anita may want to buy similar items. This could drive Anita's shopping addiction.
- Social persuasion: Anita has a number of influential people in her life – her business partner, Sam, and her friends. These people have all expressed concern about Anita's behaviour and could provide the boost in self-efficacy that she needs to address her shopping addiction. Alternatively, if they are very critical, Anita may feel unsupported, lowering her self-efficacy.
- Anita's emotional state can influence her ability to change her shopping behaviour. If she anxious, depressed or worried about money, her self-efficacy may be affected and she could be less likely to be able to address her addiction.
- Bandura's self-efficacy theory seems to be an effective tool for identifying factors that make behaviour change more or less likely for Anita. A weakness of the theory is that it is difficult to evaluate exact levels of self-efficacy and to predict how this will translate into action.
- There are other theories that could explain Anita's level of self-efficacy, such as whether she possesses an internal or external locus of control (Rotter, 1966) which could determine her addictive behaviour.

116. Discuss questions

Individual responses may include some of the following points, for example:
- The health belief model has been used to explain and understand health-related behaviours, to motivate individuals like Stacey to avoid negative health choices such as alcohol addiction, and to get better if they have already engaged in negative behaviour.

- The model identifies four factors that influence health behaviours such as Stacey's addiction to alcohol: perceived seriousness, perceived susceptibility, perceived benefits (costs and benefits) and perceived barriers.
- Stacey's behaviour was initiated as a way for her and her father to deal with grief at the loss of her mother. At that stage, perceived seriousness (such as her understanding of whether her addiction will have serious consequences in relation to her job or a life-limiting illness) might have been low. If Stacey didn't think her addiction was severe, she was less likely to seek help to quit.
- However, when she tried to give up, she found that her alcohol addiction was maintained in order to socialise with friends. She may have thought that if she continued to depend on drink, she could manage her job and be unlikely to develop an alcohol-related condition such as cirrhosis of the liver. If Stacey thought she was not susceptible to negative consequences, she was unlikely to change her behaviour.
- Stacey is now more likely to keep her job if she stops drinking. This would be a benefit. If Stacey can identify benefits of quitting, she is more likely to change her behaviour and to give up drinking alcohol.
- Perceived barriers to quitting alcohol are that Stacey drinks to be sociable with her friends, and that she may have to pay for treatment on a low salary. The more barriers that Stacey identifies, the less likely she is to change her behaviour and give up alcohol.
- Becker et al. (1978) suggest that the health belief model is useful in predicting adherence to a medical regime. It might be useful in predicting whether someone like Stacey would stick to a detox programme.
- There are other studies that are useful in assessing whether someone will adopt or reject a health behaviour, such as Rotter (1966). If Stacey has an internal locus of control she will believe she can determine the outcome for giving up alcohol. If she has an external locus of control she may believe her alcohol addiction is outside of her control and decided by external forces.

Notes

Notes

Notes

Notes

Notes

Notes